BELGIUM'S GREATEST CYCLING CLIMBS

A ROAD CYCLIST'S GUIDE TO BELGIUM'S FAMOUS 'HELLINGEN'

SIMON WARREN

F

FRANCES
LINCOLN

Frances Lincoln Limited
A subsidiary of Quarto Publishing Group UK
74–77 White Lion Street
London N1 9PF

Belgium's Greatest Cycling Climbs:
A Road Cyclist's Guide to Belgium's Famous 'Hellingen'

First Frances Lincoln edition published as *Hellingen:
A Road Cyclist's Guide to Belgium's Greatest Cycling Climbs* in 2013
This edition first published in 2016

A catalogue record for this book is available from the British Library.

978-0-7112-3806-0

Printed and bound in China

1 2 3 4 5 6 7 8 9

Quarto is the authority on a wide range of topics.

Quarto educates, entertains and enriches the lives of
our readers – enthusiasts and lovers of hands-on living.

www.QuartoKnows.com

FOR CHAR, LUX AND RYDER

Contents

A bit about Belgium

Bored of being dragged around Britain while I researched the hills for my 100 Greatest Cycling Climbs books; bored of sandwiches in the car and peering through a rain-soaked windscreen – the family decided they would put their collective foot down, 'We're going abroad next year, somewhere sunny, with a beach!'

Um, I thought, good idea. A foreign country, a different culture, exotic food, guaranteed good weather, I know! BELGIUM! You'll love it, the architecture, the steak frites, the beer, and most importantly the hills – in Belgium the hills are celebrities.

Just wait until you see The Koppenberg and The Paterberg, oh, and the Mur de Huy, you'll gasp in awe at the gradient of the Mur de Huy!

So with the family sold, and the promise of the finest steaks and an untold selection of the finest beer, come August we packed our bags and headed to the continent.

Of course it was no accident we ended up in Belgium; I'd been planning the trip in intricate detail for months. It was the logical next step after trawling through Britain for me to tackle the hills of another country. There are no mountains in Belgium, the terrain and the challenges posed by the climbs mirror those in Britain so – the Hellingen project began.

Since I fell for cycling in the late 1980s watching the Tour de France on television, I'd always wanted to ride the roads my heroes raced on. It's one of the great aspects of cycle sport, its accessibility. If you play football you can't just roll up to Anfield or Wembley for a kick about, but if you're a cyclist you can turn up to Mont Ventoux or the Stelvio Pass any day of the year and live the dream. Albeit in super slow motion and consumed with agony and dripping with sweat.

It was some time before the bergs and cols of Belgium came on to my radar though. Like most newcomers to the sport the Tour was everything, but then as I started to read more magazines, the Tour led to the Giro, which led to the Vuelta, and the plethora of one day races, notably the Classics. There are ten recognized Classics on the cycling calendar, of which five are awarded the status of the Monuments. Of these five, the two greatest are both held in Belgium, the Tour of Flanders and Liège-Bastogne-Liège. What makes these races great are the climbs, the infamous short, steep cobbles of Flanders and the yet steeper but thankfully tarmacked ramps that make up Liège-Bastogne-Liège. Over the past hundred years riders have come and gone, training methods and equipment have advanced, but the roads remain the same. The hills and valleys echo with the heroics of past champions and each year the best cyclists in the world line up dreaming of joining them.

So it is that I find myself documenting not the ordinary climbs of Britain but the famous climbs of Belgium. As you can see on the small graphic below, the country is split in two, horizontally, with Flemish speaking Flanders in the north and French speaking Wallonia in the south. This isn't a book on geography, history or politics so I'll go no further, just remember Flanders North, Wallonia South. Oh and Brussels, or to be exact the Brussels Capital Region, lies in Flanders and is officially bilingual.

I may have been kidding when I said the hills were celebrities but it's not far from the truth. Cycling is woven into the very fabric of life in Belgium. If you were asked where the home of cycling is, you may instinctively say France, or Italy, and although they have the two greatest tours, Belgium is its true home. Kids here grow up with posters of cyclists on their walls, not footballers, and to top things off it's the home of the undisputed king of cycling, Eddy Merckx. There's nothing I can add here that hasn't already been written about the great man, he dominated the sport for over a decade and excelled in every discipline, from track racing through the one day races to the Grand Tours. What I can say, though, with almost absolute certainty is that his achievements will never be equalled, he'll always be king.

With cycling holding such a place in the nation's heart, and the professional riders regarded as heroes among men it's no wonder Belgium produces so many champions. The whole country is a giant Petri dish breeding pros; you'll always see riders out training, and not just Belgians. For years it's been the number one destination for aspiring young cyclists from all corners of the globe. From Australia to Britain, those who have excelled on their domestic scenes know that to make the next step to turn professional they must make it in the melting pot of Belgian racing.

There's a race every day somewhere in this small country and each one is treated like a world championship such is the drive and ambition of those taking part. There are no easy wins, so make it here and you'll soon attract attention and be one step closer to making your dream a reality.

Of course only a tiny minority ever find themselves in this position. For the rest of us we just have our dreams, but we can ride the hills. So head to Belgium, rattle up the cobbles and weave across the painted names that adorn the infamous slopes. Once ridden you'll have a true understanding of the races and of the effort needed to defeat the Hellingen.

KEEP A
LOOK OUT FOR
OBSTACLES
AHEAD

STAY BACK
OVER THE SADDLE
FOR MAXIMUM
TRACTION

RELAX
YOUR HANDS
AND ARMS

MATCH THE TYRE
PRESSURE TO THE
CONDITIONS

Riding the cobbles

There's a right and a wrong way to ride up cobbled climbs, so here are a few tips and tricks to ease the pain. The unique set of adversities the stones present you – the lack of traction, the constant jarring and the unpredictability of what lies ahead – need a special set of skills in order to be conquered.

Let's start with traction. Traction is always a factor when climbing but when the surface under your tyres is as slippery as a snake's tongue then it's essential. To ensure the maximum rubber-to-stone contact, try to stay seated to distribute your weight evenly, with a touch of emphasis over the rear wheel where the power is transferred. When you hit a particularly rugged patch, slightly hover over the saddle to preserve the weight distribution but prevent any severe jolts from upsetting your rhythm. When the stones are wet however, or worse still wet and covered in mud, and the gradient hits 20%, well the only thing that will keep you travelling and upright is Lady Luck.

Next try to concentrate on comfort. Focus on your pedalling, keep it smooth and even to counteract the random jerking and keep your speed high so you can simply skim across the stones, rather than linger on them. Another tip is to relax. This seems very strange when your bike is being thrown from left to right, but if you slightly loosen your grip

on the bars and relax your arms they become shock absorbers, soaking up every lump and bump. Visualize yourself floating above the surface, an oasis of calm in a storm of chaos. And it's this chaos that leads me on to the next essential tip and that is to look ahead.

Unlike on a standard road where the obstacles are few and far between, on the cobbles the conditions are changing second by second. It's essential that you plot your route as far in advance as you can, look for smooth patches, places where the stones are packed close together and the gaps are well filled. However, do not, under any circumstances, unless you're a pro in a race, use the verges or concrete storm drains – that's just cheating.

Finally, consider your bike. All manner of devices have been experimented with from suspension forks to simply an extra layer of handlebar tape, but the simplest way to improve your ride is to alter your tyres. Firstly, consider a wider rubber; a couple of extra millimeters, a 25 mm or even 28 mm will provide vital extra traction. The next is pressure. If it's bone dry you'll get away with running up to 100 psi, but if it's wet you'll want to be closer to, or a touch below, 80 psi.

So with these things in mind as you hit the very first stone and you're all but thrown off the saddle, you'll know what to do. Relax, pedal smoothly, distribute your weight and keep your eyes open.

It's a long way to the top

So you'd like to ride one of the Classics? You'd like to tackle the hills in this book in their true settings – well wouldn't we all? But let's face it, that's unlikely to happen. You can't just turn up to Gent-Wevelgem or the Tour of Flanders and get a ride. Neither can you sign on at the Flèche Wallonne or Liège–Bastogne–Liège and test your legs against the best. Us mortals can but dream, we are at the bottom of the pile, or let's say the pyramid because this is how I like to picture the world of cycling, as a giant pyramid. At the base, and it's a very wide base, you have the tens of thousands of amateur races held each year, then at the top you have the Grand Tours and the Classics. Likewise for the riders, at the bottom you have anyone who's ever lined up to start a race with a number on their back, then at the top of the pile, way, way up in the clouds, you have the world's best. In order to climb up a level on the pyramid you have to succeed in the level you are at. The higher you go, the harder it gets, so the odds of you making it to the top are very much stacked against you. But there are alternatives, and number one on the list is the sportive or challenge ride. Although these events have been around for a long while it's only in the past few years that they have become a phenomenon. Where there were just a handful like the Étape du Tour that pitched riders against a stage of the Tour de France, soon there was a sportive for every occasion including the Tour of Flanders and Liège–Bastogne–Liège. Run close to the date of the race if not on the same weekend, anyone can now sign up to ride the very same course as the pros to see what it really takes. However if you don't fancy 200km of suffering but want to see how you fare against others on the climbs then there's another way. The latest development in the world of 'non competitive' cycling is that of Strava. If you own a GPS device, when you return from a ride you simply upload your data to the Strava.com website. Pretty much anywhere there is a hill there's a 'segment' and a leader board for that segment where you can compare your time to all the others who have ridden it. So head out and try your best.

> Here's a list of the key Belgian races starting with the two Monuments at the top and then descending roughly in order of significance.
>
> **Liège-Bastogne-Liège**
> **Tour of Flanders**
> **Flèche Wallonne**
> **Gent-Wevelgem**
> **E3 Prijs Harelbeke**
> **Omloop Het Nieusbad**
> **Scheldeprijs**
> **Brabantse Pijl**
> **Kuurne-Brussel-Kuurne**
> Dwars Door Vlaanderen
> Nokere-Koerse

A guide to the guide

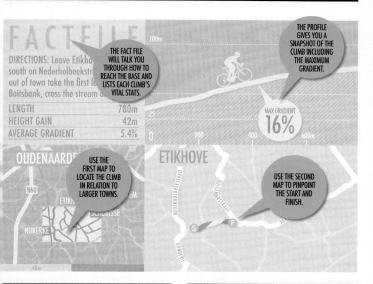

FACTFILE

THE FACT FILE WILL TALK YOU THROUGH HOW TO REACH THE BASE AND LISTS EACH CLIMB'S VITAL STATS.

THE PROFILE GIVES YOU A SNAPSHOT OF THE CLIMB INCLUDING THE MAXIMUM GRADIENT.

DIRECTIONS: Leave Etikhove south on Nederholbeekstr... out of town take the first le... Boitsbank, cross the stream a...

LENGTH	780m
HEIGHT GAIN	42m
AVERAGE GRADIENT	5.4%

MAX GRADIENT
16%

OUDENAARDE

USE THE FIRST MAP TO LOCATE THE CLIMB IN RELATION TO LARGER TOWNS.

ETIKHOVE

USE THE SECOND MAP TO PINPOINT THE START AND FINISH.

LOCATIONS

On each page you will find two maps, one showing the area the climb sits in and another that pinpoints the exact route. Although you should be able to locate each hill using these I would always recommend you take a comprehensive map of the area or a GPS/SatNav device to cross-reference.

RATINGS

The climbs are rated within the context of the book. The rating is an amalgamation of gradient, length, the likely hostility of the riding conditions and the condition of the surface. All the climbs are tough, therefore 1/10 equals 'hard', and 10/10 equals almost impossible.

MAP KEY

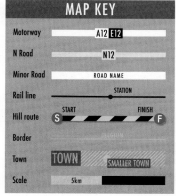

Motorway	A12 E12
N Road	N12
Minor Road	ROAD NAME
Rail line	STATION
Hill route	START ... FINISH
Border	BELGIUM
Town	TOWN — SMALLER TOWN
Scale	5km

A bit about Flanders

Flanders is the first and foremost destination for cyclists visiting Belgium. Intoxicated by the romance and drama of the cobbles they come to ride in a culture totally at one with their sport. But more than that, Flanders is the Belgium known around the world, its cities and architecture form the picture postcard images that are famous globally. It's also in Flanders where the majority of the famous races are, climaxing in the mighty Tour of Flanders, or in Flemish, Ronde van Vlaanderen.

If you head over to visit, I'd recommend making a beeline for Oudenaarde, and for one very special reason. Oudenaarde is the home of The Tour of Flanders Museum (see below). That's right, a museum devoted to a single bike race – no, it really doesn't get any better than that. The short movie you watch as you enter will have your heart pounding as history and drama from the last century to the present day bombard you across three screens. Once you wrestle your way free from the gift shop you'll be aching to hit the climbs

to rip up the cobbles like Merckx, De Vlaeminck and Boonen. My first stop after leaving was to be the Koppenberg – why not start with an absolute killer? The Koppenberg is the archetypal climb, whose name translates as 'heads mountain'. The heads (*koppen*) you see are the cobbles. In Dutch slang the stones are nicknamed *kinderkoppen*, or 'children's heads'. Not the best of images to picture as your front wheel is bouncing from one to the next.

Unfortunately, I was having to drive from climb to climb this day and as we reached the steepest part of the hill there was a film crew and a couple of old-looking guys on a tandem! They'll be lucky, I sniggered to myself. As we parked at the top I began to moan that I'd not get the shots I wanted as they'd be in the way but as time was of the essence I had to ride it so I set off to get my first taste of its gradient, downhill! As I approached the film crew, luckily they'd begun to pack up and one of them came over and stopped me.

'Hey', he said, 'You just drove up? Now you ride down?' I looked at him,

A tour of the Flanders museum will take you about two hours and it's open every day from 10am until 6pm apart from Monday when it's closed. It's also closed the second and third week of January each year. To find it just look for the orange Molteni Volvo. Also, to compliment the museum there's the café where you can sample their signature beer surrounded by cycling memorabilia and jerseys.

www.crvv.be/en/museum/museum

you're familiar, wait a minute, you're Johan Museeuw! Desperate not to look like a fraud, I told him the sob story about my lack of time, the family in tow, etc., so today I had to drive between the climbs. After some more chit-chat he wished me luck and I continued to rumble down. Twenty metres later a member of the crew came over to me. 'You know who that was?' 'Yes,' I said excitely. It was Johan Museeuw, three-time winner of Flanders and bone fide living legend in Belgium. If one man could make it up the Koppenberg on a tandem it was Museeuw, no matter who the stoker was. It was simply surreal, but I had no time to linger; I got my pics then made my way to the bottom. I had to ride up it now, and in front of a rather special audience. I half hoped they would have all packed and gone by the time I crawled past them, but then again this was a chance to show I could master the stones. I went for it, a no-holds-barred attack, seated in my 25 sprocket and going well, but alas my efforts were wasted; when I reached the top they were gone. Flanders simply oozes cycling from every corner; however unlikely his encounter was it somehow didn't feel bizarre. There are that many famous riders round here it's only a matter of time before you cross paths with one whether you recognize them or not.

Later in the year, on my final research trip I was to get another taste of the passion that cycling stirs in Flanders. This time in Geraardsbegen and a much anticipated second trip to the mighty

Muur. If any of the climbs in Flanders deserve a second look it's this one. This is the daddy of them all – it's longer, steeper, and its proximity to the end of the Tour of Flanders has made it more decisive than any other. BUT. In 2012 it was removed from the route so the organizers could send the race round a circuit and sell expensive corporate packages to VIPs in fenced off areas. Disregarding the protestations of riders old and new, journalists and most importantly the fans, they stuck to their plans, choosing profit over history and spectacle. At the summit of the Muur we bumped into a gentleman with a sandwich board over his neck. He informed us that there was going to be a mock funeral for the climb the next day and we should come along. We re-jigged our plans and sure enough, surrounded by half the town we witnessed the spectacle of local dignitaries leading a brass band playing a funeral march in front of pall-bearers and a coffin. Only in Belgium and only in Flanders would a town turn out to mourn the removal of a hill from a bike race – you've just got to love it.

limbs

ANTWERPEN

MECHELEN

BRUXELLES

HASSELT

LEUVEN

1 Kemmelberg

Gent-Wevelgem is all about The Kemmelberg. The race covers it not once but twice, and to make matters worse not only do the riders have to climb the 20% cobbles they also have to descend them on the other side. Only a handful of riders in every generation possess the awesome strength and jaw-dropping skill needed to conquer this beast and make it to the finish to contest the sprint in Wevelgem. The base departs Bergstraat on the western edge of Kemmel, and the cobblestones start the moment you hit its slopes. It's a real shock when you roll into the chaos, with stones protruding at random angles leaving huge gaping crevasses, but ride on through and a semblance of order resumes. The gradient, which is tough at first, eases back just a touch and you ride up under the cover of trees. If you are lucky enough to ride the climb in the dry you may be able to push out of the saddle, but if it's wet you'll need all your weight over the back wheel to get what little traction you can on the treacherous surface. Up ahead, the road begins its sweep left, steeper and steeper it climbs up to the 23% finale that delivers you to the plateau in front of the Belvedere restaurant. Now you must face the downhill, and take care.

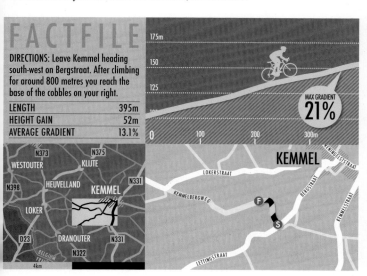

FACTFILE

DIRECTIONS: Leave Kemmel heading south-west on Bergstraat. After climbing for around 800 metres you reach the base of the cobbles on your right.

LENGTH	395m
HEIGHT GAIN	52m
AVERAGE GRADIENT	13.1%

MAX GRADIENT
21%

2 Rodeberg + Baneberg

The Rodeberg is one of the key climbs packed into the crazy finale of Gent-Wevelgem. It is quite perverse that a race featuring such wickedly steep hills is dubbed the 'Sprinters' Classic'. It may have a flat run to the line, but, boy, are the musclemen made to work for their right to fight it out. The race route travels south out of Westouter, leaving the beautiful little town across its immaculate cobbled streets, forking left on to Schomminkelstraat. You dip down, roll along the flat, then gently begin to climb up to a small tunnel of trees where the surface deteriorates and the slope really kicks up. You ride hard out into the daylight between tall hedgerows, then you're offered a slight respite up to a single house on your right from where you can see the slope ramp up in front of you. This killer drag brings you to the T-junction with the main road; the Rodeberg is finished but you're not. Turn left, pass the Berg en Sal restaurant, then immediately right ignoring the 'no entry' signs. Here to cap things off is the tiny but oh-so-vicious Baneberg. A little rise leads you left to a brutal 20% hairpin, which then leads you steep again round to the right to summit amid a collection of restaurants at the very peak of the Red Mountain.

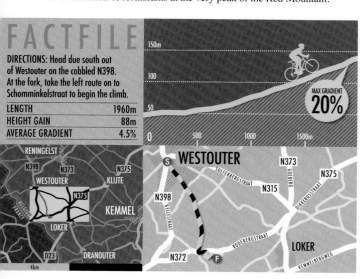

FACTFILE

DIRECTIONS: Head due south out of Westouter on the cobbled N398. At the fork, take the left route on to Schomminkelstraat to begin the climb.

LENGTH	1960m
HEIGHT GAIN	88m
AVERAGE GRADIENT	4.5%

MAX GRADIENT **20%**

3 Nokereberg

The Nokereberg is a picture-perfect, chocolate-box climb rising through the sleepy village of Nokere to the north-west of Oudenaarde. The ascent often has a small part to play in the Tour of Flanders and Kuurne-Brussels-Kuurne, but enjoys its day in the limelight when it is used for the finish of the semi-Classic Nokere-Koerse. This event started in 1944 and was originally called the Grand Prix Jules Lowie after Nokere's 1938 Paris-Nice winner, and as it has been an annual event ever since, the climb sports a permanent white line at the top painted across six rows of cobbles. The ascent starts in the centre of town just after the road begins to rise, then weaves through the beautifully neat buildings before there's a slight dip past some trees, at which point you rise again. The road is wide and the gradient mild with a maximum of 7%; the stones are packed close together and there's almost no camber to contend with. It seems far too civilized when compared with some of its more chaotic counterparts, but this is essential for a climb that's used for a sprint finish. It needs to retain a certain amount of order to allow the riders to throw all caution to the wind up the long final straight to the finish line, which comes just shy of the junction with Waregemsestraat.

FACTFILE

DIRECTIONS: Heading west from the N494 take Nokeredorpstraat into Nokere. The cobbles begin as the road starts to rise up.

LENGTH	330m
HEIGHT GAIN	17m
AVERAGE GRADIENT	5.2%

MAX GRADIENT
7%

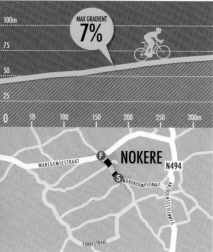

4 Kluisberg

The Kluisberg is a short but vast expanse of tarmac sweeping away from the village of Ruien up into the Doveleenbos woods. Sitting on the ridge that separates Flanders and Wallonia, the country park is home to a plethora of restaurants and gift shops. The views from the top are supreme and the bars make the most of the high ground, providing their patrons with the perfect environment to enjoy the vistas. In fact, the short distance from the foot to the summit provides all a cyclist needs. At the base there's a fantastic bike shop, Jowan Bike Technology, stocked to the rafters with the latest exotica. Next you've the challenging, but not soul-destroying, ascent; then to finish you can reward yourself with one of the world's finest beers while surveying all of south Belgium. So for the climb, on leaving the bike shop the road takes you through houses bending first right then shortly afterwards steeper left. Rounding the bend you're faced with the straight and abnormally wide road on a uniform and stiff 14% gradient. As you force your way up, the road begins to bend right through a colossal corner to deliver you to the finale. You've one final straight, slightly shallower than the earlier part of the climb but still tough up to the finish at the T-junction.

FACTFILE

DIRECTIONS: In Ruien, turn south off Grote Herreweg on to Wuipelstraat. Up to the roundabout then right on to Buissestraat to begin climbing.

LENGTH	820m
HEIGHT GAIN	62m
AVERAGE GRADIENT	7.6%

MAX GRADIENT
14%

5 Knokteberg / Côte de Trieu

Here's a climb that is ridden frequently in the Flandrian classics, which isn't actually in Flanders but in the other half of Belgium, Wallonia; hence its dual identity. The Knokteberg is its Flemish name, taken from the settlement at the top in Flanders, and the Côte de Trieu is its French name after the Wallonian hamlet at its base. Its inclusion in many races primarily provides a route back into Flanders after the riders have climbed The Kluisberg from Ruien and then descended Mont de l'Enclus. Starting among scattered farm buildings, the road works its way gently up and across some open country, and the gradient gradually increases as you approach the ridge. The nice asphalt surface seems benign when compared with fearsome cobbles, but the road soon comes into its own as you head up towards the buildings on your left. The gradient really bites here to test your legs before backing off for a short while, just long enough for you to return to your saddle in anticipation of the finale. Approaching the trees it's now steep again, then up through a right-hand bend it is harder still. Push on through, then shortly afterwards kick left and ride from under the cover of branches to finish as you leave Wallonia and re-enter Flanders.

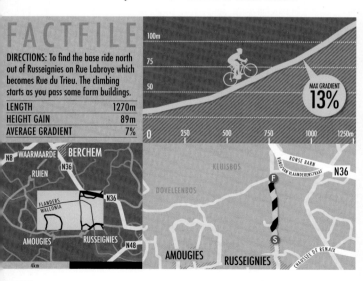

FACTFILE

DIRECTIONS: To find the base ride north out of Russeignies on Rue Labroye which becomes Rue du Trieu. The climbing starts as you pass some farm buildings.

LENGTH	1270m
HEIGHT GAIN	89m
AVERAGE GRADIENT	7%

MAX GRADIENT **13%**

6 Oude Kwaremont

This one's a real monster, it's been a cornerstone of the Tour of Flanders for generations, as well as being a defining ascent in Omloop Het Nieuwsblad and many other races. Leaving the outskirts of Berchem the climb begins on Broektestraat, and the first third is tarmac as you rise gently before a slight right turn; here the gradient kicks in and then you hit the cobbles. The transition between the two surfaces feels as if, in an instant, someone has swapped your forks for a jackhammer and your whole body is shaken to its core. The stones are large and reasonably uniform and there's a significant camber, which bulges in places, forcing gaps to appear and cobbles to dislodge. It is steep all the way to the edge of the village where you bend left and the gradient backs off, but the condition of the cobbles seriously deteriorates. Heading through Kwaremont, the road flattens; enjoy this calm because upon leaving, things turn a whole lot nastier. Now on Schilderstraat the slope increases up to a really steep ramp before it bends right. By now the cobbles are in such a bad state there's barely a metre of rideable surface; in fact, the left-hand side has all but disintegrated by the time you reach the T-junction at the top.

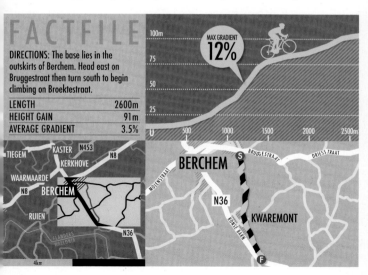

FACTFILE

DIRECTIONS: The base lies in the outskirts of Berchem. Head east on Bruggestraat then turn south to begin climbing on Broektestraat.

LENGTH	2600m
HEIGHT GAIN	91m
AVERAGE GRADIENT	3.5%

MAX GRADIENT
12%

7 Paterberg

This was the climb above all others that I had been longing to ride; there was something about its appearance that drew me to it. It's a dead straight, perfectly formed, steep line of suffering. And one that has been caught in the middle of the controversy regarding the reworking of the Tour of Flanders route. Instead of finishing in Meerbeke via The Muur and Bosberg, the organizers have devised a route that features not one but three ascents of the Paterberg. From being just a bit part, this climb is set, temporarily at least, to become the event's main attraction. It's a beautiful and brutal hill, but better than The Muur? Not in my opinion, and hopefully in a few years these last couple of sentences can be ignored. Anyhow, what is it like to ride? It's short and steep, very steep, cobbled right from the base and the further you ride the tougher it gets, with the top half a brutal 20% for a good 100 metres. The cobbles are in very good condition, though; they are large and jarring but uniform and tightly packed. At about halfway up, where the gradient really begins to bite, you'll see a faint line of cement just off centre on the wrong side of the road. It's very subtle, but just enough to smooth the gaps and provide a much better line to ride this fantastic little road.

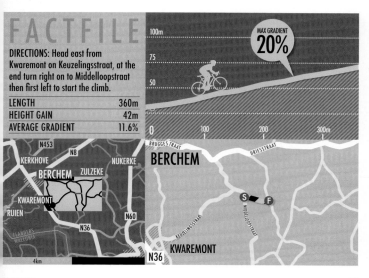

FACTFILE

DIRECTIONS: Head east from Kwaremont on Keuzelingsstraat, at the end turn right on to Middelloopstraat then first left to start the climb.

LENGTH	360m
HEIGHT GAIN	42m
AVERAGE GRADIENT	11.6%

MAX GRADIENT
20%

8 Kortekeer

Starting on a placid agricultural plain from the junction with Walkenaarsweg, Kortekeer rises ever so gently along the narrow, sandy-edged road. Leaving the tame beginning, the road kicks left in the shadow of overhanging trees then really steep right up to a maximum of 17%. Riding on the right-hand side of the road, you're forced through the apex, which only makes matters worse, or better, depending on your perspective. This climb is very reminiscent of many I have ridden in England, it has a typically English feel to it. It twists and turns, forces you out of the saddle on more than one occasion and is just thoroughly pleasant unlike all the jarring cobbles. Through the first tough right-hand bend you ride up to another set of bends, not as hard as the previous ones so you can build a little more momentum. Turning first left then almost immediately right, now with a few houses either side, and a little further up a sports field – proof they also play football and don't merely race bikes in Belgium. That's the end of the steep stuff, and you are left with no more than the final short grind up to the finish where, following a pronounced lip, the road meets a T-junction with the N60 main road just outside the village of Nukerke.

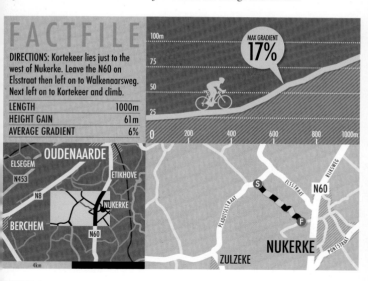

FACTFILE

DIRECTIONS: Kortekeer lies just to the west of Nukerke. Leave the N60 on Elsstraat then left on to Walkenaarsweg. Next left on to Kortekeer and climb.

LENGTH	1000m
HEIGHT GAIN	61m
AVERAGE GRADIENT	6%

MAX GRADIENT
17%

9 Koppenberg

Chaos, that's what the Koppenberg serves up, in bucket loads. It's the roughest, baddest climb in the whole of Flanders and the one that has forced more star riders to dismount than any other slope. To ride a 20% cobbled climb, one that's often wet and smeared with mud, is a skill very few cyclists possess. All it takes is for one rider to slip, stop, and unclip, then all those behind are inevitably forced to do the same. Because of this, the road has been excluded from the route many times for partial or total refurbishment, then only allowed back in when the authorities are happy. Happy that to conquer it requires athletic endeavour more than simply luck. Leaving Melden you can't miss the ominous cobbles disappearing up into the wood ahead. Things are pretty tame to begin with but approaching the trees, the action starts. As the sunlight fades it gets steeper and steeper, click down the gears but try to stay seated for that all-important traction. Exiting the canopy, the narrow road is framed with high verges, hardly perfect for the spectators who wait to see their idols either fall or conquer this beast. It continues brutally steep for a short while before there is a brief easing, then it's the final, slightly arced, and even narrower vicious ramp to the summit.

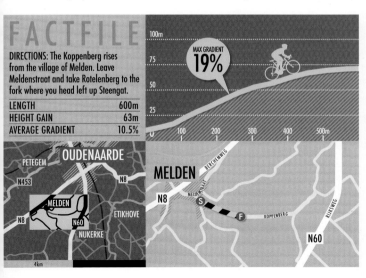

FACTFILE

DIRECTIONS: The Koppenberg rises from the village of Melden. Leave Meldenstraat and take Rotelenberg to the fork where you head left up Steengat.

LENGTH	600m
HEIGHT GAIN	63m
AVERAGE GRADIENT	10.5%

MAX GRADIENT
19%

100m
75
50
25
0

100   200   300   400   500m

OUDENAARDE
PETEGEM
N453
N8
MELDEN
N8
N60
NUKERKE
ETIKHOVE

4km

MELDEN
BEECHENWEG
N8
MELDENSTRAAT
S
F
KOPPENBERG
RIJKSWEG
N60

10 Oude Kruisberg

The Oude Kruisberg nestles in the back streets of Ronse tracing the same route up the ridge as The Kruisberg, the main N60 route out of town. This major road is wide and steep but very congested. It offers little pleasure to the rider, but will lead you to the base of the Oude Kruisberg so stick it out for a couple of hundred metres. Taking the Rue de la Croix, head away from the centre of town up to a small roundabout, head right, then ride straight across the wide road on to the concrete-slabbed back road. Away from the traffic this road is narrow, lined with parked cars, and rises gradually steeper; soon enough you reach what you came to find: the cobbles. The stones are small, smooth and slightly rounded. The gradient is mild, and this helps as it allows you to stay seated for more traction. The further you ride, though, the worse the condition of the surface. The gaps are a little wider with the odd one missing, but because of the size of the stones you'll not disappear down any holes and will have no trouble reaching the end and the junction with the main road again. To complete the journey to the summit, rejoin the main road, The Kruisberg, and ride the rest of the way out of town now on the wider, and thankfully quieter, road.

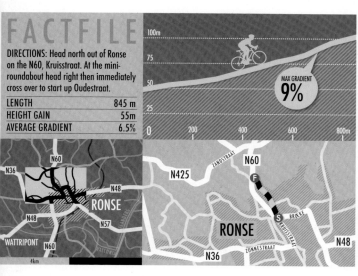

FACTFILE

DIRECTIONS: Head north out of Ronse on the N60, Kruisstraat. At the mini-roundabout head right then immediately cross over to start up Oudestraat.

LENGTH	845 m
HEIGHT GAIN	55m
AVERAGE GRADIENT	6.5%

MAX GRADIENT
9%

11 Ladeuze

Five famed climbs rise up the ridge to the south-east of Oudenaarde between the N457 in the valley and the N8 at the top. Bookended by Varent in the east and this climb, Ladeuze, in the west, you could spend all day tying yourself in knots heading up and down them in succession. The base of Ladeuze lies just outside the village of Etikhove at the point where the small road crosses the rushing Maarkebeek stream. The climb rises gently at first, up past the restaurant Ladeuze, which on race days will be full to bursting with patrons enjoying a roadside meal and waiting for the peloton to arrive. Past the restaurant and leaving behind the open fields, the gradient kicks in as you climb up towards some trees and more houses on your left. Steep and getting steeper as it climbs, work your way up to a hard right-hand bend; the road now very narrow, rugged verges begin to consume it on either side. Through the corner you continue between amphitheatre-like high grassy banks, offering spectators a perfect vantage point right on the edge of the road. The gradient eases as it climbs and soon the smooth, narrow road heads left; as the banks fade the slope peters out to level at the crossroads.

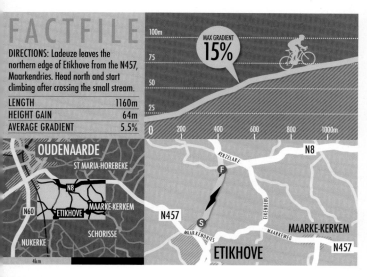

FACTFILE

DIRECTIONS: Ladeuze leaves the northern edge of Etikhove from the N457, Maarkendries. Head north and start climbing after crossing the small stream.

LENGTH	1160m
HEIGHT GAIN	64m
AVERAGE GRADIENT	5.5%

MAX GRADIENT
15%

100m
75
50
25
0   200   400   600   800   1000m

OUDENAARDE
ST MARIA-HOREBEKE
N8
N60
ETIKHOVE   MAARKE-KERKEM
NUKERKE   SCHORISSE
4km

KERZELARE
N8
F
N457
EIKENBERG
S
MAARKEWEG
MAARKE-KERKEM
MAARKENDRIES
ETIKHOVE   N457

12 Kattenberg

The Kattenberg is a work of art, its small dark stones laid out in intersecting fans with the precision of a Roman mosaic. Shimmering in the sunlight, it's so attractive you'd be happy if it were your bathroom or kitchen floor. And then you come to ride it; this hill offers the rider an experience I've not felt on any other climb. Such are the frequency of the stones and the uniform smoothness that it's not jolts which vibrate up through the handlebars but a soothing purr. This road delivers an on-the-bike massage, working out those aches and pains, vibrating the muscles at the correct frequency to leave them refreshed by the time you reach the top. OK, maybe I'm taking it a little far, but it is certainly a pleasure. In fact, the only downside is the noise cars make as they travel along its slope: it's deafening. Leaving the north-east corner of Oudenaarde the climb is on the N441, which begins as Zwijndries then, as it kinks round to the right, becomes The Kattenberg. From the right-hand bend the gradient starts to bite and it's a proper slog, regardless of the surface, up the long and uniform 8% straight to where the road begins to zigzag. The cobbles end as you head into the bends, first right, then left, right and left again, through houses where you exit as the gradient disappears.

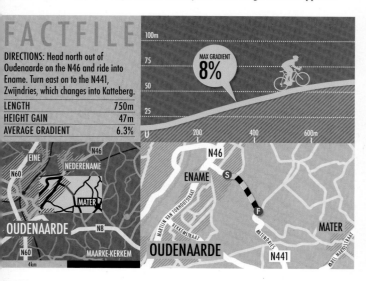

FACTFILE

DIRECTIONS: Head north out of Oudenaarde on the N46 and ride into Ename. Turn east on to the N441, Zwijndries, which changes into Kattenberg.

MAX GRADIENT **8%**

LENGTH	750m
HEIGHT GAIN	47m
AVERAGE GRADIENT	6.3%

45

13 Volkegemberg

The Volkegemberg rears out of the village of Volkegem just east of Oudenaarde and shares its base with another frequently used ascent, the Wolvenberg. Although steeper and maybe harder, The Wolvenberg cannot boast the treat that The Volkegemberg has at its crown. You start the ascent following a slight dip, then the wide, smooth, and camberless road kicks up past a small bar to settle into a challenging gradient. With a maximum slope of 12% you put the power down; the climb is not too long and looks like something you can tackle with one sustained effort. Or can you? As the road breaks left you round the corner, and bang. Cobbles. Now it's time for a new game plan, to sit down and re-think. If you've gone too deep these will hurt and break you; with the added barrage of the stones, you must leave something in reserve for maintaining momentum. They aren't the worst you will ride over in Flanders, but they are enough to shake you up and they add some true drama to the road. Once through the short stretch you're blissfully returned to tarmac and you join Rogier van Brakelstraat for the rest of the ride. Super-smooth and lined with an avenue of young trees it takes you all the way to the summit at the junction with the N441.

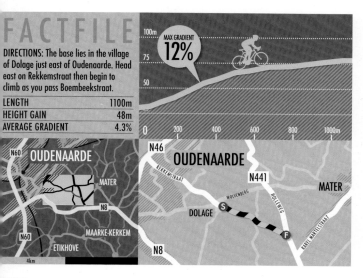

FACTFILE

MAX GRADIENT **12%**

DIRECTIONS: The base lies in the village of Dolage just east of Oudenaarde. Head east on Rekkemstraat then begin to climb as you pass Boembeekstraat.

LENGTH	1100m
HEIGHT GAIN	48m
AVERAGE GRADIENT	4.3%

14 Eikenberg

The Eikenberg is long at over 1.5 kilometres, and although never too steep (with a maximum gradient of just 10%), the ferocity of the surface more than compensates for the kindness of the slope. Starting at the junction with Borgtstraat, the narrow single-track road bends gently upwards and away to the left. There's no warm-up as you're on the cobbles right away. The further you ride, the larger the stones, and worse still, the greater the gaps between them. At around halfway, where the road kinks left, you briefly leave the cobbles and hit a patch of incredibly poor tarmac – welcome relief from the consistent jarring. Make the most of whatever even surface you can find because you're soon back on to the stones; thankfully, smaller, smoother ones, and set closer together they are much easier to ride, but they don't last. If you were reasonably comfortable then sorry, that's about to end as the nice neat stones make way for ones that feel like upended bricks. As the road kinks right then left through some trees, you'll feel every single one as your very joints are shaken apart and you struggle to keep hold of the bars. This amazing road comes to an abrupt halt on reaching the T-junction at the top, where the transition to asphalt never felt so good.

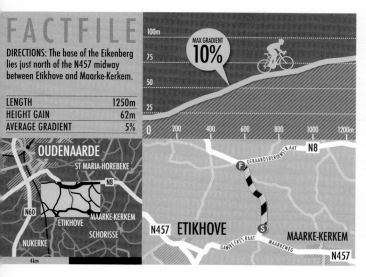

FACTFILE

DIRECTIONS: The base of the Eikenberg lies just north of the N457 midway between Etikhove and Maarke-Kerkem.

LENGTH	1250m
HEIGHT GAIN	62m
AVERAGE GRADIENT	5%

MAX GRADIENT 10%

100m
75
50
25
0   200   400   600   800   1000   1200m

OUDENAARDE
ST MARIA-HOREBEKE
N8
N60
MAARKE-KERKEM
ETIKHOVE
SCHORISSE
NUKERKE
4km

N8
GERAARDSBERGENSTRAAT
F
N457 ETIKHOVE
MAARKE-KERKEM
GANSBEEKSTRAAT
MAARKEWEG
N457

15 Taaienberg

Taaienberg translates literally as Tough Mountain and although it's no Alpe d'Huez it is certainly tough enough – tough enough for it to be an almost permanent fixture on the Tour of Flanders route since 1974. In fact, it's a regular in many races including the semi-Classics E3 Prijs and the Omloop Het Nieuwsblad. Add to this that it has become known in recent times as multiple Classic winner Tom Boonen's favourite climb, and you have one of the best venues for a pain fest in the whole region. To get a taste of it for yourself, head for the base at the southern tip of Etikhove. Leave the village on Nederholbeekstraat then turn sharp left back on to Boitsbank. Cross the stream and the slope rises, at first on a concrete road; round the left-hand corner and you head towards the cobbles. They are massive, and when you hit them they really throw you around; on top of that it is steep, really steep, up to a leg-breaking 18% under the trees. In its favour, though, the camber is very slight and if you've had enough of the cobbles there's a concrete gutter running along each edge offering some relief for those who require it. Exiting the trees the gradient backs off as the road bends gently right and, although still on punishing cobbles, levels up to the join with Bossenaarstraat.

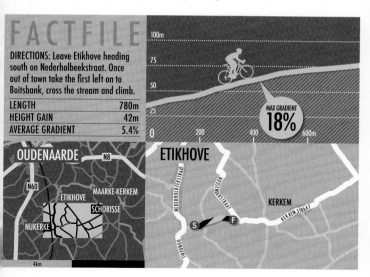

FACTFILE

DIRECTIONS: Leave Etikhove heading south on Nederholbeekstraat. Once out of town take the first left on to Boitsbank, cross the stream and climb.

LENGTH	780m
HEIGHT GAIN	42m
AVERAGE GRADIENT	5.4%

MAX GRADIENT
18%

100m
75
50
25
0
200   400   600m

OUDENAARDE   N8

N60

MAARKE-KERKEM

ETIKHOVE
SCHORISSE

NUKERKE

4km

ETIKHOVE

NEDERHOLBEEKSTRAAT
BOSSENAARSTRAAT
KERKEM
KERKEMSTRAAT
DONDERIJ
S   F

16 Kanarieberg

The Kanarieberg is a linchpin of the semi-Classic Kuurne-Brussels-Kuurne run on the last Sunday of February or the first Sunday in March each spring. Following Omloop Het Nieuwsblad (held on the Saturday before), it kicks off the season of cobbled classics, which last for the next six weeks culminating in the Paris-Roubaix. These earlier races don't boast as fearsome a roll-call of climbs as the Tour of Flanders, they just offer up a few tasters – hors d'oeuvres before the main event. You approach the Kanarieberg from the N48 and from a higher vantage point you see the formidable sight of the road ramping up the ridge in front of you. Drop down to the base, round a handful of farm buildings and you are ready to climb as the road eases up, bending slightly left and right. From its placid beginning the slope soon increases as you embark on a long, leg-sapping straight at the end of which the road kinks right and the gradient bites hard. This stinging little rise will stay in your legs for the rest of the ascent as you weave upwards past more buildings. The slope eases a little for you to recover then ramps up again continuing to bend slightly left and right to finish at the T-junction in front of a large restaurant in the Muzikbos forest.

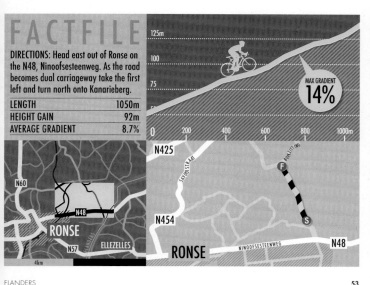

FACTFILE

DIRECTIONS: Head east out of Ronse on the N48, Ninoofsesteenweg. As the road becomes dual carriageway take the first left and turn north onto Kanarieberg.

LENGTH	1050m
HEIGHT GAIN	92m
AVERAGE GRADIENT	8.7%

MAX GRADIENT
14%

17 Boigneberg

The Boigneberg is a climb that features the other typically Belgian road topping: concrete. Laid in sections usually measuring 4 to 5 meters, at the end of each one you hit the join – thump. It's a small thump, but on a long road they begin to wear you down, and the constant, metronomic hindrance to your progress makes settling into a rhythm incredibly hard. As soon as you are comfortable you are jolted and lose a fraction of your speed. This is particularly evident uphill where your momentum is all-important in keeping you on top of your gear. On the plus side, though, the surface has charm, and the Boignberg would not be the climb it is without this topping, one that was laid over its original cobbles back in 1979. Sharing its base with the Kapelleberg, which heads off to the left, the climb starts from the top of Kabuizestraat and heads right, then straight away bends 90 degrees left. Tarmac at first, the concrete begins after a ridge in the road that almost throws you from your seat. Climbing dead straight you pass a small white chapel on the left and it is steep, up to 15%. The climb eases the further you ride and bears left, twisting and climbing some more to eventually top out at the point where the concrete ends and you are returned to tarmac.

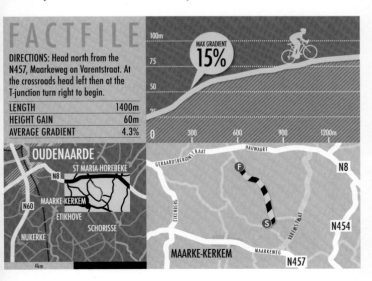

FACTFILE

DIRECTIONS: Head north from the N457, Maarkeweg on Varentstraat. At the crossroads head left then at the T-junction turn right to begin.

LENGTH	1400m
HEIGHT GAIN	60m
AVERAGE GRADIENT	4.3%

MAX GRADIENT 15%

100m
75
50
25
0   300   600   900   1200m

OUDENAARDE
ST MARIA-HOREBEKE
N8
MAARKE-KERKEM
N60
ETIKHOVE
SCHORISSE
NUKERKE
4km

GERAARDSBERGSESTRAAT
HAUWAART
F
N8
EIKENBERG
VARENTSTRAAT
S
N454
MAARKE-KERKEM
MAARKEWEG
N457

18 Foreest

The Tour of Flanders has only flirted with Foreest but many other events have been keen to include its slope in their parcours. Hills fall in and out of favour as organizers experiment; mistakes are made, and improvements found to construct the perfect race route. Until 2012 the mighty Tour of Flanders followed a similar format, travelling west to east from Brugge to Meerbeke, but the next venture was to incorporate a circuit finish, based around the mighty Paterberg. You start the climb on Hessestraat heading east away from the village of Schorisse. The road is level for a few hundred meters then you feel it gradually rise under your tyres as you approach the junction with Beekkantstraat. From here on it is tougher, bending gradually right through open fields before heading into a set of bends up under the cover of trees. First left then creeping right out from under the branches before bending hard left, the narrow road rising up through houses. Ahead the road bends left, steep left, feeling tougher than the advertised 13%. This hard corner then leads you on to a rougher broken surface as the roots of tall trees force their way up through the tarmac. The ascent ends as the road bends and climbs right up through a group of farm buildings to summit at a crossroads.

FACTFILE

DIRECTIONS: Leave the village of Schorisse heading east away from the N454 on Essestraat. Essestraat becomes Hessestraat, then you start to climb.

LENGTH	930m
HEIGHT GAIN	60m
AVERAGE GRADIENT	6.5%

MAX GRADIENT
13%

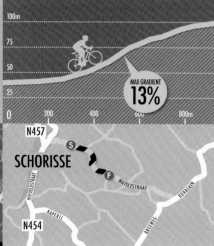

19 Molenberg

The cobbles of The Molenberg resemble waves at sea in a force ten gale! Where there was once order there is now only chaos. Stones protrude at random angles, gaps appear from nowhere to swallow your front wheel and, on top of that, the camber is so pronounced, children could sledge down it in winter. The base to this mayhem is an inconspicuous turning resembling a private driveway next to a sign for the Mechelse Koekoek restaurant. Head up over a bridge, pass the restaurant then the bedlam begins as the slope rises towards a right-hand bend. The road is just wide enough for a single car, and on the left there is a metre of dirt should the cobbles be just too disorganized for you. Round the corner and the condition of the surface deteriorates further; whoever laid these stones obviously had not done a corner before! For the next 100 metres you are at war with the topping as the slope reaches its maximum gradient of 14%. Things do gradually improve as you reach the end of a long hedge, the gradient drops and the surface becomes a touch more regular. Continue on cobbles up round the left-hand bend, keep easing further left, then you are returned to tarmac for the final few metres before the slope disappears.

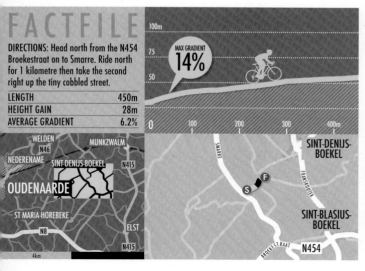

FACTFILE

DIRECTIONS: Head north from the N454 Broekestraat on to Smarre. Ride north for 1 kilometre then take the second right up the tiny cobbled street.

LENGTH	450m
HEIGHT GAIN	28m
AVERAGE GRADIENT	6.2%

MAX GRADIENT
14%

100m
75
50
0   100   200   300   400m

WELDEN
N46
MUNKZWALM
NEDERENAME
SINT-DENIJS-BOEKEL
N415
OUDENAARDE
ST MARIA-HOREBEKE
N8
ELST
N415
4km

SMARRE
SINT-DENIJS-BOEKEL
FRANKOUTER
SINT-BLASIUS-BOEKEL
BROEKESTRAAT
N454

20 Leberg

A proper vicious climb that has a build-up as uncomfortable as you're likely to find. Flanders may be best known for its cobbled climbs but there are also a number of stretches of flat cobbles or pavé, dotted around the landscape. These can add that little bit more spice to a race, and one particularly evil stretch – The Haaghoek – takes you right to the base of The Leberg. As with the approach to all climbs, position in the peloton is key; you need to be at the head of the pack to cover the moves and avoid the bottlenecks that form on the narrow roads. So battling to reach the front before a major ascent is vital, and it takes special talent to do so on these lumpy stones. With your body now feeling like the flesh has been shaken clean off the bones you return to tarmac, dip down and pass a large parking area to begin the climb. The gnarled road snakes like a wizard's walking stick, first left, then right, left, right, steeper and steeper up through the houses. It's a short climb, requiring one massive effort to ride through the slopes that reach a maximum gradient of 13%. As the road arcs right up to a crossroads, the worst of the gradient is behind you and now it's a much milder affair, but one that only fades away completely when you reach the junction with Pottenberg.

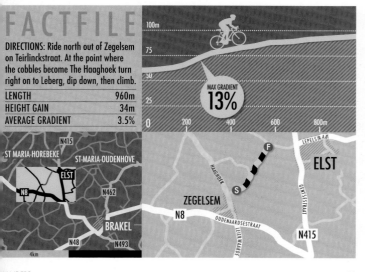

FACTFILE

DIRECTIONS: Ride north out of Zegelsem on Teirlinckstraat. At the point where the cobbles become The Haaghoek turn right on to Leberg, dip down, then climb.

LENGTH	960m
HEIGHT GAIN	34m
AVERAGE GRADIENT	3.5%

MAX GRADIENT
13%

21 Valkenberg

To find the base, leave Brakel heading north on Kerkhofstraat crossing a small clearing to the bridge over Kouterbeek. The asphalt surface isn't perfect, it's scarred and cracked like it has been baked at too high a temperature, but you would choose this over either cobbles or concrete slabs any day. Head over the stream, and following a slight plateau the climb begins as you pass the junction with Wederspad on your left. It's a serious gradient, up to 13%, as the road becomes Valkenbergstraat and kinks right then left up to the café Venus. One sure-fire sign that you're riding a Flanders hill is that if there isn't a bar at the top there will be at least one on its slopes. The Belgians love their beer as much as they love their bikes and what on any normal Sunday would be a sleepy establishment, on race day will be bulging at the seams. The locals will all be straining to keep an eye on the TV right up to the point when they can rush outside and witness the action in the flesh. Of course there's no stopping for the riders so for them it's up past the bar then round to the left, the road lined with giant concrete drainage slabs. Past a small white chapel the climb has one more right-hand kink before it peaks at the brow just shy of the junction with Valkenstraat on the right.

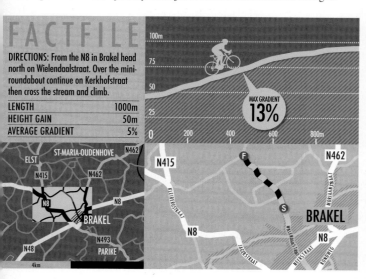

FACTFILE

DIRECTIONS: From the N8 in Brakel head north on Wielendaalstraat. Over the mini-roundabout continue on Kerkhofstraat then cross the stream and climb.

LENGTH	1000m
HEIGHT GAIN	50m
AVERAGE GRADIENT	5%

MAX GRADIENT
13%

22 Tenbosse

A simple residential street – steep, but unremarkable in almost every other way. Such is the power of cycling and its great events that even the most unlikely of roads can, once a year, maybe more often, become stadiums lined with screaming fans – who like their entertainment laced with pain and gruelling effort, who want the deciding moment of the race to unfold before their eyes, on their hill. The climb of Tenbosse had until 2012, been added at the business end of the Tour of Flanders on the run in to Geraardsbergen leaving the town of Brakel. The base is where Tenbossestraat meets Dr De Drijverestraat and you see the climb rear up in front of you. The near-perfect surface, as smooth as rolled icing, kinks only very slightly right then left. Like the direction, the gradient offers little deviation. At a steady 10% it is steep enough to force you out of the saddle, but not to have you in any trouble. With nowhere to grab a moment's respite, this uniformity of gradient can often be a rider's undoing as they are required to maintain an intense effort from base to summit. As you reach its finish, there is a slight kick as you approach the junction with Kruisstraat, then the road levels as it becomes Olifantstraat and it's on to the next quarry.

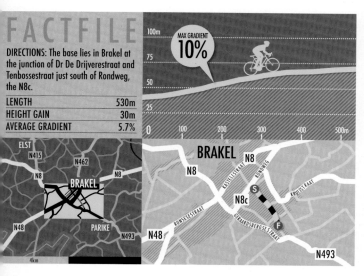

FACTFILE

DIRECTIONS: The base lies in Brakel at the junction of Dr De Drijverestraat and Tenbossestraat just south of Rondweg, the N8c.

LENGTH	530m
HEIGHT GAIN	30m
AVERAGE GRADIENT	5.7%

MAX GRADIENT **10%**

23 Berendries

Berendries' lack of notoriety and charm is its greatest weapon. In your mind, before an event, you prepare for the highlights – for the climbs that have earned the big reputations. You read the preview, you trace the route, you focus on the key battlegrounds; however, it's all those between that often do the damage, and this climb falls into that category. A regular on the Flanders route for many years, the slope begins as you cross the small stream leaving the village of Michelbeke. The road is narrow, asphalt, and lined with the familiar concrete drainage gutters. The gradient is mild to begin then as you bend round to the right it begins to ramp up. Ahead, your course is now dead straight, lined either side with houses and visibly increasing in gradient up to a maximum of 12%. Just shy of a fake brow, the increase is so pronounced it's as if the road has been picked up, placed over a giant's knee, bent, and then put back in place. This ramp will really sting your legs up to the junctions at either side, then it eases, kinking slightly right then shortly after, a more pronounced left. The top is not far now and the gradient gently ebbs away as you roll to a finish, adjacent to Kapittel on the left, just shy of the junction with the N462.

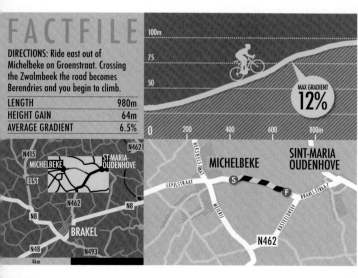

FACTFILE

DIRECTIONS: Ride east out of Michelbeke on Groenstraat. Crossing the Zwalmbeek the road becomes Berendries and you begin to climb.

LENGTH	980m
HEIGHT GAIN	64m
AVERAGE GRADIENT	6.5%

MAX GRADIENT
12%

24 Muur-Kapelmuur

To the people of Geraardsbergen The Muur is the Tour of Flanders and since its first inclusion in 1950 it has become one of (if not the most) iconic sights in the whole of the sport. The Muur isn't simply a single street, though – it is a twisted amalgamation of cobbled roads that begins as you ride through the market square and rumbles up past the cathedral. After passing the cathedral, turn left on to Vesten and the stones are so perfectly set you'll hardly notice them as you climb gently upwards to where the real action begins. Turning sharp right you join Oudebergstraat and now you're on the proper cobbles. It's no more Mr Nice Guy as you meet Belgium's finest attempt to shake your hands from the bars. Next the road (if you can call it that) banks sharp right, eases back for a short stretch, then bends 90 degrees left into one of the most demanding stretches of climbing you're likely to face. Forcing the pedals through each revolution, searching for traction, you reach the top and turn left. Now ready yourself for the cherry on top – The Kapelmuur – arguably the most photographed piece of road in the history of cycling. This 50-metre cobbled curve, rough, rugged, and as steep as hell, delivers you to the summit at the base of the Chapel. You've made it.

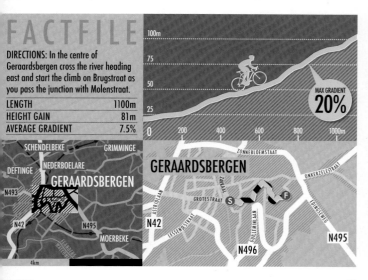

FACTFILE

DIRECTIONS: In the centre of Geraardsbergen cross the river heading east and start the climb on Brugstraat as you pass the junction with Molenstraat.

LENGTH	1100m
HEIGHT GAIN	81m
AVERAGE GRADIENT	7.5%

MAX GRADIENT
20%

25 Bosberg

For many years the Bosberg was the final hurdle – or in most riders' cases, the final nail in the coffin – before the run into the finish of the Tour of Flanders. If you've not got a sprinter and haven't previously dropped your rivals then this would be your last chance to make your move, to take your place on the roll of honour. To start, leave the centre of Atembeke, a short way out of Geraardsbergen, and head east, climbing gently on the concrete slabs to the slight right-hand curve at the base of the cobbles. Hit them with all the speed you can muster. This is one for the big ring, and the aim is to float over the crowns of the stones like a powerboat skimming the crests of waves. Apart from the slight kink at the base, the road is straight and wide, a grand cobbled avenue surging through a small wood. The gaps between the stones occasionally expand and contract to accommodate the odd deformation and there's a slight camber, but you will have no trouble riding it as, on the whole, the surface is well set and well maintained, befitting the protected status that the road acquired in 1993. This climb can really flatter the mortal rider so give it full gas and imagine the bar at the crest to be packed with fans as you leave the cobbles and switch back to level concrete.

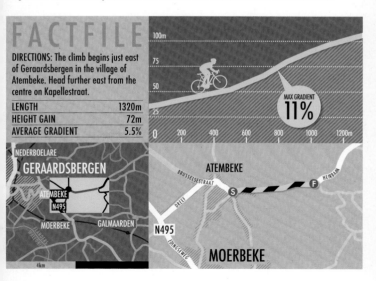

FACTFILE

DIRECTIONS: The climb begins just east of Geraardsbergen in the village of Atembeke. Head further east from the centre on Kapellestraat.

LENGTH	1320m
HEIGHT GAIN	72m
AVERAGE GRADIENT	5.5%

MAX GRADIENT
11%

NEDERBOELARE
GERAARDSBERGEN
ATEMBEKE
N495
MOERBEKE GALMAARDEN

4km

ATEMBEKE
BRUSSELSESTRAAT
DREEF
N495
EDINGSEWEG
HERBORN
MOERBEKE

Slippery
when wet

Once you've digested the climbs of Flanders, to finish the first half of the book here's a spotter's guide to the infamous cobbles. I say cobbles, but technically that's an incorrect moniker. A cobble is actually a naturally occurring stone, one retrieved from a river bed that has been rolled smooth and round by millennia of rushing water. It was these raw building blocks that were employed as the first replacement for dirt roads, packed in tightly to form an incredibly hard-wearing, all-weather surface. Very few of these roads still exist and if you've ever attempted to ride across one you'll find it's all but impossible. Following a modest advance in stone masonry, however, the cobble was ultimately replaced, and the sett was born. Cut to size, with or without accuracy, the sett is a purpose-built block designed to pave a road. This revolutionized road building at the time but as you will see on the following pages there seems to be no standard shape, size or material. The majority are cut from granite, but some, such as those on the Koppenberg below, are simply shaped from an assortment of roughly similar sized stones. So there you have it, a sett is the correct word but cobble is the word that has stuck, and anyway, a 'setted climb' just doesn't have the same ring as a 'cobbled climb'. Now peruse the following pages, study the surfaces, then, when quizzed you'll be able to instantly tell your Kemmelberg from your Koppenberg.

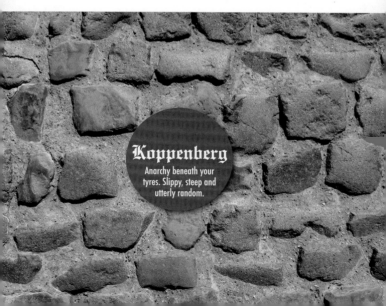

Koppenberg

Anarchy beneath your tyres. Slippy, steep and utterly random.

Kattenberg

Smooth as a baby's
bum and as neat as
a tailored suit.

Taaienberg

Aggressive stones that will
thump your front wheel
like a boxer pounding
a punch bag.

Kapelmuur

Perilously slick with vast irregular gaps and a healthy amount of foliage.

Oude Kruisberg

Small, neat and even, but with cavernous divisions waiting to swallow you up.

Muur

Irregular, slimy,
covered with debris,
and jagged like
shark's teeth.

Paterberg

Imposing, boulder-like
stones, set in lines as
uniform as the gradient
is vicious.

Eikenberg

A smorgasbord of cobbles from large and rounded to small and vicious like upturned bricks.

Nokereberg

Ordered, manicured, but a far-from-benign rumble fest.

Bosberg

As neat as a stone carpet, but with a slight camber and a few defects to add some spice.

Oude Kwaremont

From fearsome camber through ordered chaos to total disintegration.

Molenberg

Stones? They are more like asteroids floating in space. It's like trying to ride over Stonehenge.

Kemmelberg

Regular and large, worn icy smooth with a shine like a lizard's skin.

A bit about Wallonia

Wallonia is a region of contrasts, you have the beautiful rolling hills of the Ardenne which in the right weather are breathtaking. Then on the flip side you have the industrial grime of the cities and it's in these opposite environments that my two favourite races are held, Liège-Bastogne-Liège and Flèche Wallonne.

Although I love the cobbles of Flanders, my body just isn't suited to them, I don't have the muscular frame needed to soak up the constant punishment. No, give me the smooth slopes of the Ardenne any day, and the steeper the better. When I arrived, the hill I couldn't wait to ride, the one that had the hairs on the back of my neck standing up and my heart racing, was the Mur de Huy, it's more than just a hill, it's an icon. Emblazoned with the Huy logo from base to summit, this short and vicious road is hallowed ground for cyclists. As I began my ascent I felt honoured, privileged to be there, would my legs be able to do it justice, how hard could it really be? I was shocked. Before now I'd only seen it on television, it looked tough but not that tough. In real life it's immense. It's pretty stiff up to the corner at half way but after this, well this is where it gets serious. The remaining distance to the plateau is as unrelenting

and brutal a stretch of road as you'll find anywhere. To win up the Mur de Huy you need an intimate knowledge of its slope twinned with unbelievable strength. The list of riders who've attacked too early and died a thousand deaths within sight of the finish line could fill another book. Flèche Wallonne contains many other great climbs, but there's no hiding that they are all just leg softeners for the main event. Like Gent-Wevelgem in Flanders where it's all about the Kemmelberg, Flèche Wallonne is about the Mur de Huy, oh, and it's ridden three times during the race for good measure.

If Flèche Wallonne is all about one climb, though, Liège-Bastogne-Liège, known simply as La Doyenne 'The Oldest', is all about the sheer number and frequency of its hills. Again and again they hit you, each one with its own character, its own nuances, each one a star in its own right but together they form a megastar.

The race travels south from Liège and there's a long warm up before the first hostilities begin as you pass through La Roche-en-Ardenne but this initial climb is little more than a wake-up call on your way to the turn in Bastogne. It's on the way back that the race comes alive and the next climb on the menu was the next climb I'd longed to ride, the iconic Côte de Saint Roch in Houffalize.

My first and most vivid memory of

the Belgian Classics is a photo from an old copy of *Winning* magazine. It was taken on the Côte de Saint Roch and pictures the multicoloured peloton blending in, all but merging with the watching crowd. A river of riders flowing up the impossibly steep urban climb, banked by the fans, five deep, their stomachs held in to avoid contact. It's a blur of activity, a spectacle unmatched in any sport or arena where athletes and onlookers form a unison. Neither could exist without the other it's a perfect symbiotic relationship.

Leaving Houffalize the race then continues its journey north, and following another short hiatus the riders approach Stavelot. From now on it's full bore. The order and frequency of the climbs will vary from year to year but the result is always the same – pain. From the Côte to Stockeu, through the mighty Col du Rosier via the Côte de la Redoute to the Côte de Saint-Nicolas and everything in between. Only the most gifted, or let's say 'the best prepared' riders will triumph. Let's face it, and although it's the unwritten law to brush talk of doping under the carpet, the role-call of recent winners is hardly a glowing endorsement for the sport. Between 1999 and 2007, seven of the eight winners have been banned for drug taking, and either side of this exceptional time span

there are plenty of riders who have been implicated in scandal yet avoided prosecution. As with the Grand Tours and the almost impossible amount of mountains they now climb, is Liège simply too tough to win clean? Do you need to be 'juiced up' to defeat its vicious parcours? We can only hope that the very recent winners in what is regarded as one of the cleanest periods in cycling for generations have clearer consciences than their predecessors.

Let's leave it there, though, and get back to the hills. On my travels to ride the ascents featured in the famous races I also couldn't help checking out some other roads I'd noticed, and I felt they must be included in the book. The massive climb up to the Signal of Bretange, the highest point in the whole of Belgium, had to be on the list. And then there's the Col du Haussier, rated as the toughest climb in the whole of the country; the Mur de Huy aside, I think I'd agree. I then took off on an excursion to the very south of the country to check out the hills around Bouillon and found two crackers: Les Enclaves and Vielle Route de France. So when heading to Belgium, don't end your visit in the north – head south to find some 'proper' hills. Although Flanders often takes the spotlight, Wallonia is more than a match, and in many ways offers superior riding.

LA REDOUTE

1892 - 1992
COMMUNE D'AYWAILLE

LIÈGE - BASTOGNE - LIÈGE

TOURNAI

MONS

CHARLEROI

26 Côte de Haut-Bois

This twisting climb rises from the tiny village of Haltinne, through a small patchy wood to the slightly larger village of Haut-Bois up a terribly scarred surface. You begin at the T-junction on a corner where the Rue du Vivier Traine leaves the N941 and heads south. You'll hardly notice the slope at first as you make your way past small fields and houses, but leaving the last buildings behind it begins to rise up. Ripped to shreds by agricultural vehicles, the climb gently makes its way up to the first left-hand bend then into the trees where it totally falls apart. Bearing right into a small clearing then bending left, the gradient kicks up to its maximum, just a touch over 10%. Not brutally steep, but hard going when you take into consideration the abrasive tarmac under your wheels. Twisting left, then right, and rougher still into a dark tunnel of trees, grind your way up and the slope eases to all but level out as you head towards the light. Out into a clearing you now kink right and up steep once more before bending gradually left, not as tough, but just as rough. Fix your eyes on the yellow sign for Haut-Bois, and use this to drag you the final few metres to the finish, a thin white line painted across the road just shy of a collection of farm buildings.

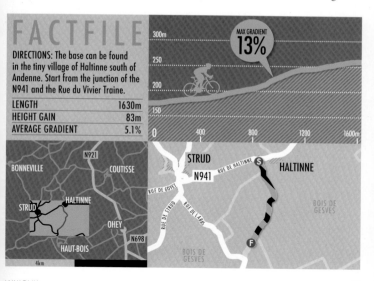

FACTFILE

DIRECTIONS: The base can be found in the tiny village of Haltinne south of Andenne. Start from the junction of the N941 and the Rue du Vivier Traine.

LENGTH	1630m
HEIGHT GAIN	83m
AVERAGE GRADIENT	5.1%

MAX GRADIENT **13%**

300m
250
200
150

0   400   800   1200   1600m

N921
BONNEVILLE   COUTISSE
STRUD   HALTINNE
OHEY
HAUT-BOIS   N698
4km

STRUD
N941   RUE DE HALTINNE   HALTINNE
RUE DE GOYET
RUE DE STRUD   RUE DE LABIS
BOIS DE GESVES
BOIS DE GESVES
S
F

27 Côte de Groynne

Rising from the neat stone buildings in the small village of Strud, the Côte de Groynne takes you up over the ridge, through Groynne and down into Andenne. The base lies at a fork, where the road splits left and right either side of a narrow brick building with a small shrine at its base. Take the left fork on the smooth surface, then sweep round a left-hand bend into a long straight with a couple of slight kinks in it. You will certainly know you're climbing, but the gradient is no killer as you approach a forested area with trees either side of you. For some reason there is a line across the road here and the gradient increases a touch more; conifers on your right, deciduous on your left, you flow upwards to level opposite a left-hand junction. Following a small ramp up through the last of the trees it's time to leave their protection and complete the ascent across exposed farmland. The road cuts its way as straight as an arrow up to the brow of the sparsely grassed ridge, past two large clumps of trees on the left standing like massing armies. It's not just the gradient but the elements you'll be fighting now, with nothing to shelter behind; pray that the wind is blowing in your favour as you aim for the summit, a painted line across the road next to the sign for Andenne.

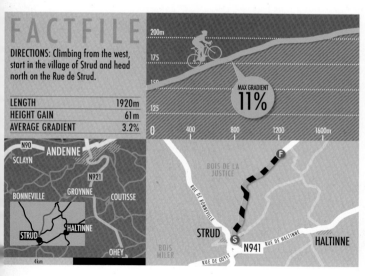

FACTFILE

DIRECTIONS: Climbing from the west, start in the village of Strud and head north on the Rue de Strud.

LENGTH	1920m
HEIGHT GAIN	61m
AVERAGE GRADIENT	3.2%

MAX GRADIENT
11%

200m
175
150
125
0   400   800   1200   1600m

N90
ANDENNE
SCLAYN
N921
BONNEVILLE   GROYNNE   COUTISSE
STRUD   HALTINNE
OHEY
4km

BOIS DE LA JUSTICE
RUE DE BONNEVILLE
STRUD
BOIS MILER
S   N941   RUE DE HALTINNE   HALTINNE
RUE DE GOYET
F

28 Côte de Peu d'Eau

Although the Mur de Huy is where La Flèche Walloone is decided, it doesn't mean the other climbs on the route don't have a part to play in the outcome. It's in the maze of hills that sit between Huy and Andenne where the rider's legs are softened, making ready for the big finale. The base of the Côte de Peu d'Eau lies in the centre of Andenne but the race joins it half way up via the Rue des Aguesses at the apex of the second large left-hand bend. To truly experience the road, you must of course begin at the base, where the N921, signposted to Ciney, heads up a narrow road to a 90-degree left-hand bend. Through this corner you weave gradually left before sweeping right, up a substantial gradient that I'd rate at just a touch below tough. Following this right-hander you enter a straight-up to the next right where the race route joins from the left, then, over some rippled tarmac, it's right up to a slight brow and a levelling. Ahead you see the road arc up and away, it's straight, wide and there is nowhere to hide. Aim for the white garage up ahead of you – use this as your carrot – as after here the road kinks slightly left and the gradient abates. You have just the final few hundred metres now to finish across a pedestrian crossing – there the road levels.

FACTFILE

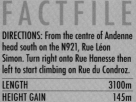

DIRECTIONS: From the centre of Andenne head south on the N921, Rue Léon Simon. Turn right onto Rue Hanesse then left to start climbing on Rue du Condroz.

LENGTH	3100m
HEIGHT GAIN	145m
AVERAGE GRADIENT	4.7%

MAX GRADIENT
12%

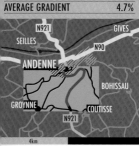

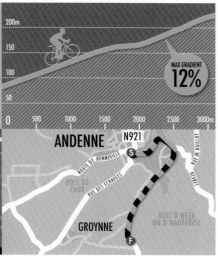

29 Côte de Bohisseau

The Côte de Bohisseau is a fearsome little climb heading south out of Andenne, and one the town is rightly proud of – so much so they've permanently emblazoned their web address 'Andenne.be' across its surface at regular intervals from base to summit. Leaving the N90 you start the ascent from a small plaza outside a tiny church and rise gently up the Rue de Perwez to a pedestrian crossing just shy of a crossroads. Carrying straight on, the slope is suddenly steep, very steep, as the narrow road squeezes its way through the houses. There's the slightest change in direction, but alas no easing in severity until you pass the junction with the Rue des Chalées where the slope starts to back off, then all but level, at the base of the Rue Pelémont. Now you may be tempted by this vicious-looking street, but it's not the road you're searching for and will only lead you into a cul-de-sac, so carry straight on. Upwards, through the traffic-calming measures and parked cars, you reach the next significant stretch of climbing. Not as harsh as the opener but hard enough to have you clicking down a number of sprockets, it delivers you to the finale. Twisting left and right, the road winds steeper again to exit Andenne, leading on to the finish across the ubiquitous white line.

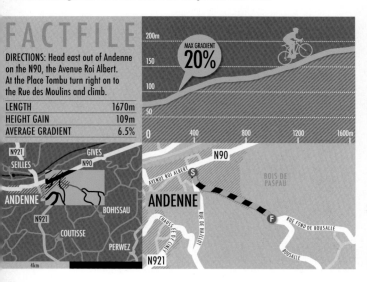

FACTFILE

DIRECTIONS: Head east out of Andenne on the N90, the Avenue Roi Albert. At the Place Tombu turn right on to the Rue des Moulins and climb.

LENGTH	1670m
HEIGHT GAIN	109m
AVERAGE GRADIENT	6.5%

MAX GRADIENT
20%

30 Côte de Ereffe

Ride away from the N641 across a small bridge, then begin the climb up into a tunnel of trees. It's a steep kick up the narrow road then once free of the trees, where a small track heads straight on, the road breaks left and the slope increases. These are the roughest stretches of the climb, get through them and you'll have no worries later on. Following a short straight you bend right; an Armco barrier frames the pitted, broken road, and once again you are surrounded by trees. Round to the left the scenery opens up and you can see the climb unfold in front of you. The surface is now smoother and the slope shallower as you approach a couple of houses; here you bend slightly right then straighten before weaving through the buildings that punctuate the length of the road at regular intervals. The gradient is relatively gentle until you reach a 90-degree left-hander and it increases significantly as it bends up and around a lumpy, grassy mound. A short straight is followed by a 90-degree left, then, all but levelling, you head out across the ridge of an open plain with wonderful views on both sides. Up ahead there's a bold, white water tower that marks the summit. Make your way up into the centre of Marchin and finish across the white line.

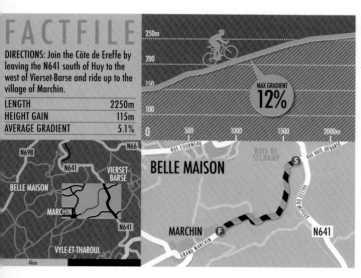

FACTFILE

DIRECTIONS: Join the Côte de Ereffe by leaving the N641 south of Huy to the west of Vierset-Barse and ride up to the village of Marchin.

LENGTH	2250m
HEIGHT GAIN	115m
AVERAGE GRADIENT	5.1%

MAX GRADIENT
12%

250m
200
150
100
0   500   1000   1500   2000m

N698
N66
N641
RUE FOURNEAU
BOIS DE SÉCHAMP
RUE HAIE DE BARSE
VIERSET-BARSE
BELLE MAISON
BELLE MAISON
MARCHIN
N641
VALLÉE DU HOYOUX
S
MARCHIN   F
N641
GRAND MARCHIN
VYLE-ET-THAROUL
4km

31 Mur de Huy

First of all I must apologize to all those riders I've screamed 'ATTACK!' at while watching Flèche Wallonne on TV. 'GO! NOW!!' I bellow, but no more. Now I will simply sit in awe of their efforts as they battle this monster of a road. Vicious doesn't even come close, and it's some climb simply to reach the base. The slope up through Huy will have your heart rate peaking even before you veer off the main road, bold graphics branded on the road ushering you on to the Mur. Narrow and steep through houses, the logo repeated at first every 10 metres draws you upwards to bend right, then steeper left towards one of the most famous corners in cycling. Epically steep, veering up round the grassy mound with the Huy emblems now just a metre apart. This is the backdrop of a thousand photos, but it is nowhere near the top and this is what shocked me. What comes next is enough to break any rider and it's the reason I will cease to heckle. This climb is far tougher than it looks on TV. Attack too soon and you blow, leave it too late and your rivals are gone: timing is everything. On and on, gradually bending left, it's purgatory to reach the arena in front of the church where you can collapse a victor, or a victim, of the mighty Mur de Huy.

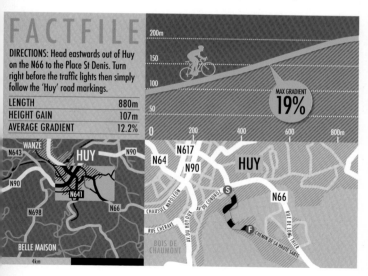

FACTFILE

DIRECTIONS: Head eastwards out of Huy on the N66 to the Place St Denis. Turn right before the traffic lights then simply follow the 'Huy' road markings.

LENGTH	880m
HEIGHT GAIN	107m
AVERAGE GRADIENT	12.2%

MAX GRADIENT **19%**

32 Les Enclaves

Buried in a forest at the base of Belgium, close to the French border lies the wicked little climb of the Col du Sati, or Les Enclaves. It's a punishing grind from base to summit and one that gives you little chance to use your saddle as you wrench your bike up the slope. The base lies in the calm surroundings of a secluded picnic area on the banks of a rushing river. Climbing from a bridge across a tributary you sweep round to the right and the road rears up into the thick trees. It is seriously steep, close to 20%, and there's no respite until the very top. The slope does ease the further you climb, but the effort you put in at the base will never leave your legs. Engage a low gear and don't head off too hard; crawl along the smooth narrow surface beneath the tall conifers. The road straightens up then begins a gentle meandering left and right, but there are no corners, just slight deviations in direction. Suffer your way along, stick to the task, enjoy the effort, and hold out for the trees to part and for the open sky to return. As the sky brightens you bend left for the final stretch up to the brow on the horizon. Once over this you are just left the task of rolling to the finish at the pale yellow chapel under a brace of trees at the junction with the road into Bouillon.

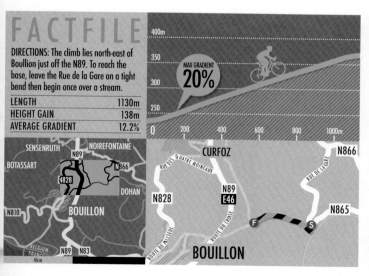

FACTFILE

DIRECTIONS: The climb lies north-east of Bouillon just off the N89. To reach the base, leave the Rue de la Gare on a tight bend then begin once over a stream.

LENGTH	1130m
HEIGHT GAIN	138m
AVERAGE GRADIENT	12.2%

MAX GRADIENT 20%

33 Vielle Route de France

The Vielle Route de France looks as if it's sneaking out of the back door of Bouillon, a narrow, rough road making a run for the border with France. Standing at its base opposite the Hotel de France are what look like the remains of a once-grand stone gatepost – a fitting marker for a road that leads to another country – but now overgrown and forgotten. Steep from the base, the road ramps up in the shadow of towering vegetation and past buildings clinging to its edge then bends right slightly before straightening again. Soon you're high above the town and river below, the gradient backs off a touch but not enough to make it any easier as you continue through the houses along the rough and pitted surface. Bending slightly right again you embark on another arduous straight, and the slope doesn't give an inch until you catch sight of a large white building with a Mexican-themed mural on its side. Pass this and there's a brow, reach it and you can settle into some easy climbing through a 90-degree bend before – past a lone house – it ramps up again to the next brow just shy of a radio mast. The road now appears flat, but you're still climbing and as you reach the trees that cap the summit you've one final tough push to top out and roll over into France.

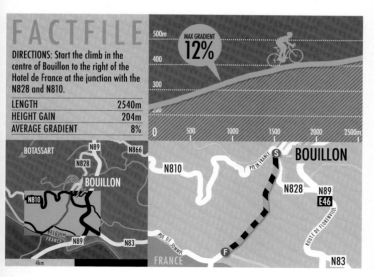

FACTFILE

DIRECTIONS: Start the climb in the centre of Bouillon to the right of the Hotel de France at the junction with the N828 and N810.

LENGTH	2540m
HEIGHT GAIN	204m
AVERAGE GRADIENT	8%

MAX GRADIENT **12%**

34 Côte de La Roche-en-Ardenne

This long and beautifully winding road leaves the picturesque paved square in La Roche-en-Ardenne and heads south on the N834. Setting off up the wide, smooth surface, you climb gently, bending first right then left. The gradient is mild throughout, and you may well feel the need to get out of the saddle now and again to refresh the legs, but on the whole this climb can be comfortably tackled sitting down. Cutting its way along the precipitously steep valley side you'll find yourself riding in the shadow of the trees to your left, but level with the tops of those on your right. The higher you climb the more the road meanders, echoing the lower slopes of an Alpine pass as it snakes its way through the thick forest onwards and upwards. It's a true pleasure to ride: in and out of the smooth bends then, before long, the trees begin to thin out. Patches of open land start to appear and you head into three pronounced bends, first sweeping right, then left, then right once more; exit this final curve and the road straightens to reveal a brow ahead. The slope kicks up marginally here to ensure you have to work a little bit harder to reach the brow, but once over, the incline ebbs away and the climb evaporates on the high plateau.

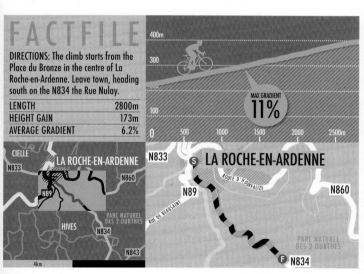

FACTFILE

DIRECTIONS: The climb starts from the Place du Bronze in the centre of La Roche-en-Ardenne. Leave town, heading south on the N834 the Rue Nulay.

LENGTH	2800m
HEIGHT GAIN	173m
AVERAGE GRADIENT	6.2%

MAX GRADIENT **11%**

𝕲𝕺𝔩 𝖉𝖊 𝕳𝖆𝖚𝖘𝖘𝖎𝖗𝖊

Well here it is, the toughest climb in Belgium. Forget the cobbles of The Koppenberg or the vicious gradient of the Mur de Huy, this climb has all that, and much more – it's just brilliant. Start your adventure in the shadow of a giant church on the neat cobbles of the Rue de Moulin; short and sweet, they are just enough to rough up your legs before you hit the next section. Resembling the Côte de Saint-Roch, the perfectly smooth road rears up close to 20% skimming past the doorways that butt up to its edge. Push on through and the slope eases as you leave the town behind and enter the forest. Now much rougher, you round a giant boulder that dictates the course of the road, and then you reach a large cemetery. Climbing round its high stone walls you briefly dip down then bend left on to a super-steep ramp. Grind upwards, level in front of a children's play area, then climb gently again before a second, this time longer, descent. At the base there's a junction, head left and climb once more, on and on; it's a relentless, arduous slog up a punishing gradient, made even worse by the rough surface. Now deep in the forest the road bends 90 degrees left and you've made it, just roll along the final few metres to the large sign that marks the summit.

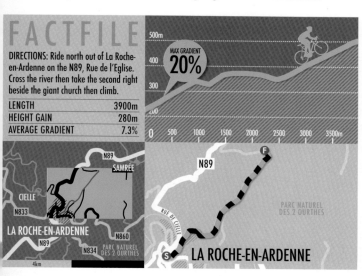

FACTFILE

DIRECTIONS: Ride north out of La Roche-en-Ardenne on the N89, Rue de l'Eglise. Cross the river then take the second right beside the giant church then climb.

LENGTH	3900m
HEIGHT GAIN	280m
AVERAGE GRADIENT	7.3%

MAX GRADIENT
20%

500m
400
300

0   500   1000   1500   2000   2500   3000   3500m

N89
SAMRÉE
CIELLE
N833
LA ROCHE-EN-ARDENNE
N89
N860
N834   PARC NATUREL
DES 2 OURTHES
4km

N89
F
RUE DE CIELLE
PARC NATUREL
DES 2 OURTHES
S   LA ROCHE-EN-ARDENNE

36 Côte de Saint-Roch

Chances are, if you've only ever seen one photograph of Liège-Bastogne-Liège, then this is where it was taken. The iconic view of the peloton en masse, climbing this fearsome slope, the riders from gutter to gutter merging with the thousands of flag-waving fans, is one of the truly classic images of cycling. The colour, the passion, the severity of the slope amplified by its proximity to the houses is a sight that encapsulates the sport as well as, if not better than, any other. Start the climb from the Rue de Bastogne near an old Second World War tank and it's steep from the off. Head up the vertical ribbon of tarmac that parts the houses; after a couple of hundred metres it backs off slightly and you bend left. Now you're about to begin the most famous stretch. Ahead, the straight road butting up to people's doorways will max out at a vicious 20% before easing. Aim for the visible crest, reach this and that's the worst of it over; the slope returns to more like the 14% advertised at the base and you ride through the last of the houses. You've still a long, long way to the finish and your final goal is the white chapel that lies in the shadow of two giant radio masts. Grind your way up to roll over the line both exhausted and exhilarated.

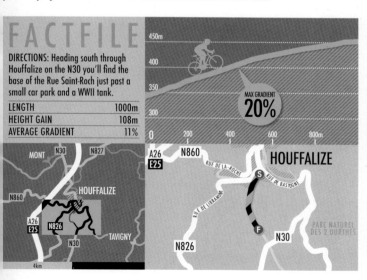

FACTFILE

DIRECTIONS: Heading south through Houffalize on the N30 you'll find the base of the Rue Saint-Roch just past a small car park and a WWII tank.

LENGTH	1000m
HEIGHT GAIN	108m
AVERAGE GRADIENT	11%

MAX GRADIENT
20%

450m
400
350
300
0
200   400   600   800m

MONT   N30   N827

N860

HOUFFALIZE

N860

A26
E25   N826

N30   TAVIGNY

4km

A26
E25   N860   RUE DE LA ROCHE   HOUFFALIZE

S   RUE DE BASTOGNE

RUE DE LIBRAMONT

F

N826   N30

PARC NATUREL
DES 2 OURTHES

37 Côte de la Vecquée

Do all roads lead to Stoumont? Judging by the multitude of signs that clutter the base of the Côte de la Vecquée you could believe you had arrived at the very centre of Belgium. The climb technically starts at the junction, but for the full effect you should begin from the banks of the River Amblève in the bottom of the valley. Heading up into Stoumont you reach the garish intersection and beneath the direction signs turn sharp left. Steep from the start you bend left some more before straightening up so you can take in the view through the gaps between houses. Up to and round the bend ahead, the gradient bites a little more, but you'll be able to keep on top of your gear; you just need to apply a touch more pressure. Until you reach the next bend there is no change in the slope; in fact, it is all but uniform now for some distance, allowing you to focus on your pedalling, to focus on the mechanics of your body as you tap out a smooth and efficient rhythm. Round a solitary house you're now heading back the way you came, then you bend right up through some houses and back into forest. In and out of trees the slope becomes almost unnoticeable up to the point where it fades away completely, opposite a left-hand turning around a left-hand bend.

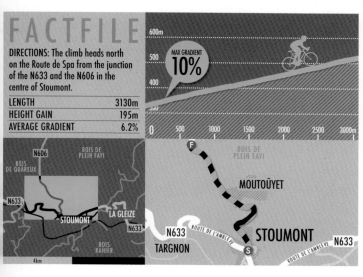

FACTFILE

DIRECTIONS: The climb heads north on the Route de Spa from the junction of the N633 and the N606 in the centre of Stoumont.

LENGTH	3130m
HEIGHT GAIN	195m
AVERAGE GRADIENT	6.2%

MAX GRADIENT
10%

38 Côte de Wanne

This climb is a beast. It will wear you down on the lower slopes, then, when you're tired and vulnerable, it comes in for the kill. You begin as you leave the region of Grand-Halleux, winding left and right through a couple of gentle bends you find yourself at the base of a remorseless and arrow-straight 10% ramp. Grind your way up, and up, until you finally can take a breather amid the bespoke houses that litter the hillside. This respite doesn't last. As you enter the village of La Vau the gradient kicks up again, steeper as you negotiate the narrow road between tall hedgerows to meet a small junction. Be wary of traffic coming from your left and head straight on, trying to preserve your momentum to climb harder still on the punishing slope. Only when you exit the village do things become easier, and, on your left, through the gaps in the trees, you can view the beautiful scenery. Next you reach a junction where you head right and ride round into the forest, the slope is a touch easier again and the climb leads you to a sweeping left-hand bend into a grand avenue of trees. Riding under the canopy the gradient ebbs away, and you can build up some speed to attack the final rise, exiting the forest to cross the familiar white line and finishing just shy of the village of Wanne.

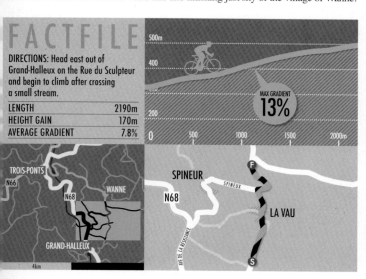

FACTFILE

DIRECTIONS: Head east out of Grand-Halleux on the Rue du Sculpteur and begin to climb after crossing a small stream.

LENGTH	2190m
HEIGHT GAIN	170m
AVERAGE GRADIENT	7.8%

MAX GRADIENT
13%

500m
400
200
0   500   1000   1500   2000m

TROIS-PONTS
N66

WANNE

N68

GRAND-HALLEUX

4km

SPINEUR

SPINEUX

N68

LA VAU

AVE DE LA RESISTANCE

F

S

39 Côte d'Aisômont

Heading south out of Trois-Ponts, the Côte d'Aisomont can't boast any fearsome gradient, but it still has a few tricks up its sleeve to test a rider's legs. You begin the climb on the Rue de la Gare on a stretch of the infamous Belgian concrete slabs. The slope is shallow and the surface smooth, but the slight jolt you receive every 5 metres when you hit the divides punctuates your rhythm, then every 100 metres there's a narrow strip of cobbles just to add a little more spice. As you reach the railway station this novel collection of surfaces ends and the now-tarmacked road bends left across the railway lines, then right to the base of a sharp hairpin. The ascent is now testing as you round the corner and head into forest, past a few houses then bending right through the majestic, tall conifers. Stretching out in front of you, the uniform slope kinks slightly left then through a traffic-calming chicane into another long straight that takes you away from the trees on to open land. As you climb you can enjoy the fantastic views over the rolling hills before easing ever so gently, the slope delivers you into the small village of Aisomont. Exiting, the gradient kicks up through more traffic calming for a final flourish to the finish line opposite a large car park on the left.

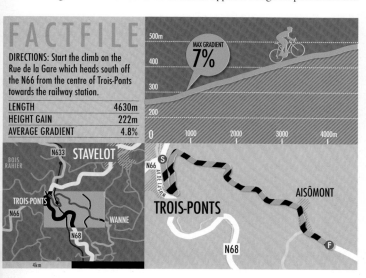

FACTFILE

DIRECTIONS: Start the climb on the Rue de la Gare which heads south off the N66 from the centre of Trois-Ponts towards the railway station.

LENGTH	4630m
HEIGHT GAIN	222m
AVERAGE GRADIENT	4.8%

MAX GRADIENT
7%

40 Côte de Brume

On a clear day the views from the top of the Côte de Brume are arguably the most spectacular in Belgium, trouble is, it's one hell of a climb to get there. Leaving the centre of Trois-Ponts you begin the ascent on the Rue des Villas. Weaving a little you're brought to the first of three hairpins, the gradient easing as you sweep left, before increasing as you exit and head for the second. This time steeper, bend right and you're immediately thrust into the third and final deviation before embarking on the arduous slog to Brume. Whereas the corners on the lower slopes distract you from the effort, nothing will help you now as you grind up across the abrasive surface. It is no killer, not quite hard enough to force you out of the saddle, but steep enough to make you uncomfortable in it. As you reach a large clearing under giant pylons you're allowed a substantial rest, and it is perfect timing as the worst is just ahead. Bending right the slope kicks up, twisting and turning into the village of Brume; now you'll be out of the saddle as it touches its wickedly steep maximum of 20%, past a small chapel. Push on through and the fierce slope, thankfully ebbing away, delivers you to the summit at a small triangle of grass where at last you can stop to admire the vista.

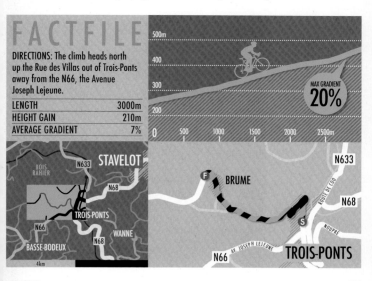

FACTFILE

DIRECTIONS: The climb heads north up the Rue des Villas out of Trois-Ponts away from the N66, the Avenue Joseph Lejeune.

LENGTH	3000m
HEIGHT GAIN	210m
AVERAGE GRADIENT	7%

MAX GRADIENT
20%

41 Côte de Stockeu

To mark his five wins in Liège-Bastogne-Liège, the Côte de Stockeu is now affectionately known as 'Stèle Eddy Merckx', and to celebrate this there's a sculptural monument to the great man at its summit. Like Merckx, this road takes no prisoners – it chews riders up and spits them out, barely wide enough to ride three abreast and with a surface like the face of the moon. Leaving Stavelot, south, across a cobbled bridge, take the road ahead of you that veers slightly off to the right. Smooth at first and very steep from the start you ride up and up through the houses, straight, bending right, straight, then right again. So far so good, but now the road bends left, you exit Stavelot and it really gets nasty. At the junction with a cobbled track the road narrows, the topping falls apart, and the gradient ramps up to an evil 20% if not steeper. Under the cover of trees, inch upwards trying to pick out a clean line, trying to stay on top of your gear to enter a clearing where both the surface improves and the slope eases. But this calm doesn't last for long as the road ramps up again, a short sharp kick back into the trees for the rugged finale up to the famous statue. It is here you join the main road to continue right and upwards for some time until the incline disappears.

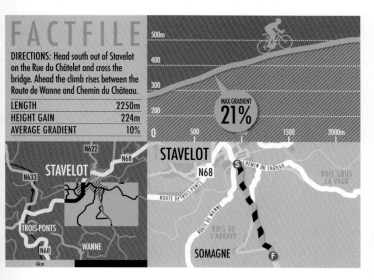

FACTFILE

DIRECTIONS: Head south out of Stavelot on the Rue du Châtelet and cross the bridge. Ahead the climb rises between the Route de Wanne and Chemin du Château.

LENGTH	2250m
HEIGHT GAIN	224m
AVERAGE GRADIENT	10%

MAX GRADIENT
21%

500m
400
300
200
0

0   500   1000   1500   2000m

N622
N68
STAVELOT
N633
STAVELOT
N68
CHEMIN DU CHÂTEAU
BOIS SOUS LA VAUX
ROUTE DE TROIS-PONTS
TROIS-PONTS
ROUTE DE WANNE
BOIS DE L'ABBAYE
WANNE
N68
SOMAGNE
S
F
4km

42 Côte de la Haute Levée

This road incorporates the most intense, claustrophobic and cycling un-friendly traffic-calming measures I've ever encountered. Leaving the beautiful cobbled streets of Stavelot you cross the Rue Marlennes and straight away it's steep: 13% right from the junction. You then reach the monumental concrete barriers that dissect this road, squeezing all traffic together with no room to move or chance of escape. Trapped, your natural reaction is to get out, so you up the pace making an already tough climb one hell of a lot harder. Approaching a left-hand junction, the full width of the surface is painted blood-red and the corners edged with vivid chevrons – it is the very definition of an eyesore. Next comes the brief, but welcome, relief of a passing place; you can exhale, relax for a moment, before plunging back into the narrowing once more. Thankfully at the apex of the next long left-hand bend, the barriers finish and, free, you climb steep round to the right and the slope eases off. Levelling before it climbs again, the rest of this long slope is pretty mild. Through another set of divides either side of a roundabout you then continue towards Spa until the gradient eventually evaporates adjacent to a solitary stone farmhouse.

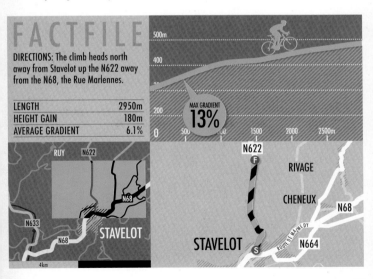

FACTFILE

DIRECTIONS: The climb heads north away from Stavelot up the N622 away from the N68, the Rue Marlennes.

LENGTH	2950m
HEIGHT GAIN	180m
AVERAGE GRADIENT	6.1%

MAX GRADIENT
13%

500m
400
200

0   500   1000   1500   2000   2500m

RUY N622
N68
N633
N68   STAVELOT
4km

N622
F
RIVAGE
CHENEUX   N68
ROUTE DE HAUTE DY
STAVELOT   S   N664

43 Mont Rigi

There aren't many countries whose highest point can be reached by bike, but Mont Rigi does just that, taking you to the Signal de Botrange, the very geographical peak of Belgium. Start your ascent in the centre of Malmedy and climb gradually upwards out of the valley and away from the hum of the Spa racetrack. Rising gently at first, the snaking road eases its way into Beverce where it briefly levels. There's no major gradient yet, but you're constantly rising, and once through the village you enter the Hautes Fagnes-Eifel natural park. Round a hairpin and across a small bridge you're climbing through thick forest, the road now a tangle of tarmac weaving through the trees. The gradient ebbs and flows through the endless twists and turns and there's barely 50 metres of straight until you leave the village of Mont. But once through, the sky opens up and you're free of the barrage of bends, to continue to the summit on the grand avenue that inches upwards across this epic scenery. Through the forest to where the road kinks right, then traversing the open plateau of the High Fens, the road leads you to bend left and drop down. Pass the Mont Rigi sign then at the junction bear right for the final few hundred metres to finish at the bar under the stone tower.

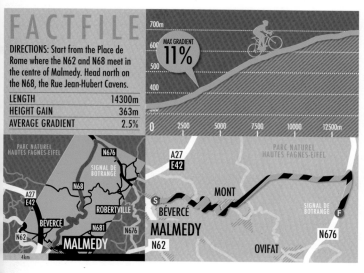

FACTFILE

DIRECTIONS: Start from the Place de Rome where the N62 and N68 meet in the centre of Malmedy. Head north on the N68, the Rue Jean-Hubert Cavens.

LENGTH	14300m
HEIGHT GAIN	363m
AVERAGE GRADIENT	2.5%

MAX GRADIENT
11%

44 Col du Rosier

Liège-Bastogne-Liège is the climber's classic, the one-day race where the mountain men, those who excel in the grand tours, can leave their mark on the spring's events. Hitting the riders in a relentless frenzy the climbs are steep and short, but one that certainly breaks the mould is the Col du Rosier. This twisting ascent is as close to a mountain road as you'll find in Belgium; it's a proper climb and one that cannot be conquered with brute force alone, you need to be a lightweight. The gradient is tough from the start, riding out of Ruy, winding upwards you reach a jumble of bends, the road, concertinaed upon itself. Pull yourself upwards; meandering through the thick forest the gradient eases enough for you to click up a couple of sprockets. On and on you climb to reach a 90-degree left in front of a scattering of houses, you cross a stream then continue straight, always climbing. Entering Andrimont, the gradient increases significantly, but once free of the buildings it relents enough for you to make the long way to the T-junction, where you bank hard right. The finale is played out on the larger main road and you peak at the line that marks the end of hostilities and the beginning of the hair-raising descent down into Spa.

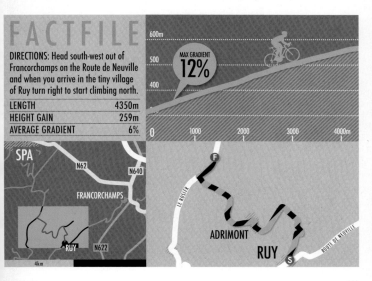

FACTFILE

DIRECTIONS: Head south-west out of Francorchamps on the Route de Neuville and when you arrive in the tiny village of Ruy turn right to start climbing north.

LENGTH	4350m
HEIGHT GAIN	259m
AVERAGE GRADIENT	6%

MAX GRADIENT
12%

600m
500
400
0   1000   2000   3000   4000m

SPA
N62
N640
FRANCORCHAMPS
N62
RUY   N622
4km

LE ROSIER
F
ADRIMONT
RUY
ROUTE DE NEUVILLE
S

45 Col du Maquisard

Given the choice I'd pick short and steep over long and steady any day; my heart lies on a stretch of rugged 1-in-3, not a mild mannered 1-in-10, but I'll make an exception for this climb. The Col du Maquisard is such a pleasure to ride, packed full of bends that flow one into the next, and never too steep, allowing you to tap out a rhythm all the way to the summit. It's like a snapshot of an alpine road that has had the sting taken out of it and been transposed to Belgium. Heading off, you climb the Rue de Vieux Pré away from the Rue Marteau towards the initial deviations, first left, the gradient easing, then hard right, the centrifugal force pulling you round and slinging you out. Next into a long left-hand bend, the slope kicks up a touch and you're delivered on to an open plane. The road snakes across the grassland weaving left and right and a little steeper up toward the forest. Once amongst the trees, the surface deteriorates a little as you make your way to the next majestic bend. This expansive hairpin, levelling at the apex and edged with crisp white lines, pulls you round, then propels you upwards into the trees. Ahead, the pristine surface weaves through the tall conifers, the uniform gradient rounding a final clearing to summit in front of a small park.

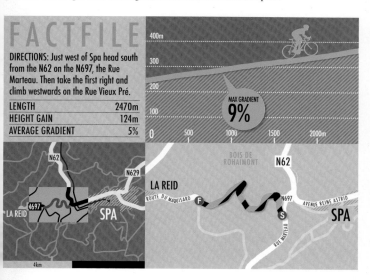

FACTFILE

DIRECTIONS: Just west of Spa head south from the N62 on the N697, the Rue Marteau. Then take the first right and climb westwards on the Rue Vieux Pré.

LENGTH	2470m
HEIGHT GAIN	124m
AVERAGE GRADIENT	5%

MAX GRADIENT
9%

400m
300
200
100
0   500   1000   1500   2000m

N62
N629
N697
LA REID
SPA
4km

BOIS DE ROHAIMONT
N62
LA REID
ROUTE DU MAQUISARD   F
N697
AVENUE REINE ASTRID
S
RUE MARTEAU
SPA

46 Mont Theux

A mountain? Well that is stretching it a bit, there are no real mountains in Belgium; in fact, the closest genuine mountain must be over 400 kilometres away. Start from the mini-roundabout on the edge of Theux and head up the wide, smooth and – I can't deny – busy road, ramping up to a substantial 10% gradient. Approaching, and riding through a sweeping left-hand bend, the tarmac is rippled, wavelike; it's almost nauseating for a while as you leave Theux behind. Level in front of a large graveyard then dipping before the real work begins. The slope kicks up hard, rising into Mont, you pass the village sign then the road bends right and you're allowed a final rest. The slope all but levels through the village then coming up next is a horrible incline. Bending left then straightening, the road disappears to a point on the horizon, a dead-straight line of 12% suffering: uniform in width, uniform in gradient, uniform in the way it wears you down as you attempt to keep on top of your gear. If your best isn't enough to keep up with the other riders, there's nowhere to hide, no corner, no deviation, just the strength-sapping slope that you'll only love when it finally ebbs away.

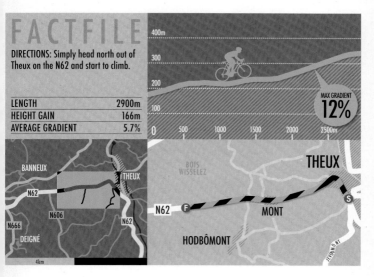

FACTFILE

DIRECTIONS: Simply head north out of Theux on the N62 and start to climb.

LENGTH	2900m
HEIGHT GAIN	166m
AVERAGE GRADIENT	5.7%

MAX GRADIENT
12%

400m
300
200
100
0   500   1000   1500   2000   2500m

BANNEUX
THEUX
N62
N606
N62
N666
DEIGNÉ
4km

BOIS WISSELEZ
THEUX
N62 F
MONT
HODBÔMONT
S

47 Côte de la Redoute

This classic climb is proof that even the most unlikely of roads can work their way into cycling folklore, and La Redoute, named after a battle in the Franco-Austrian War, is a true monument of the sport. Coming at the business end of Liège-Bastogne-Liège it takes no prisoners as it sieves through the peloton leaving only the freshest and strongest to tackle the run in to the finish. I lost my way a couple of times as I negotiated the tangled streets of Sougné-Remouchamps, but once you've wrestled yourself free of town you're on the right track when you see the motorway bridge over the road ahead. Next turn right on to a featureless narrow road and climb parallel to the motorway on your right before heading left to the small La Redoute monument. From here on in it gets interesting. The road narrows, twists slightly, then, covered in the painted names of riders, really begins to ramp up. Kinking right then left, crushingly steep, you have to fight the bike to keep your momentum and reach the brow where the punishing 20% slope eases. You are still far from the top, though, and with your legs burning you have to push on as the narrow road squeezes through the hedgerows bending gradually right then sharp left, finally to summit under a radio mast.

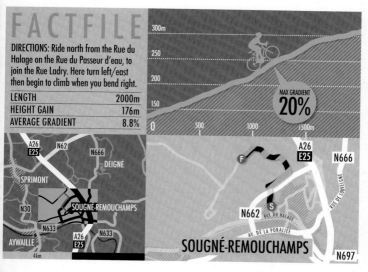

FACTFILE

DIRECTIONS: Ride north from the Rue du Halage on the Rue du Passeur d'eau, to join the Rue Ladry. Here turn left/east then begin to climb when you bend right.

LENGTH	2000m
HEIGHT GAIN	176m
AVERAGE GRADIENT	8.8%

MAX GRADIENT **20%**

48 Côte de la Roche aux Faucons

It would make sense to tackle this climb riding the Rue d'Avister from its base, but Liège-Bastogne-Liège attacks it in a slightly more convoluted way. Cross the river on the Rue du Pont, head left across a large expanse of tarmac then right over railway lines. You see the road weaving upwards into the forest ahead as you bend right then left before settling into a long straight, the Avenue des Ormes. Beautifully smooth, the road appears to disappear into a hole in the trees ahead, but before you reach them you take a left on to the Avenue de Hony. The gradient backs off and you gather yourself before joining the Rue d'Avister. Turning right it is steep and rough, you wind left, then right, then left, snaking upwards dodging the potholes and cracks. There's little chance to find a rhythm and it's far from picturesque as you reach your next obstacle, a concave storm drain running bizarrely, right across the road. Once negotiated, continue onwards through the trees to reach a noticeable brow where you're afforded a breather. The slope eases beside an open field then bears left, the further it turns the steeper it gets on a much smoother surface. The final ramp is a proper leg stinger, and you finish the climb riding across the famous names painted all the way to the summit.

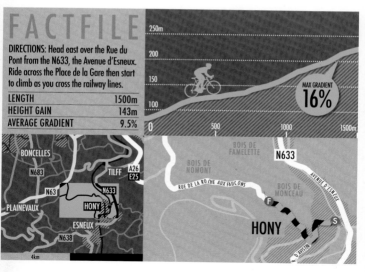

FACTFILE

DIRECTIONS: Head east over the Rue du Pont from the N633, the Avenue d'Esneux. Ride across the Place de la Gare then start to climb as you cross the railway lines.

LENGTH	1500m
HEIGHT GAIN	143m
AVERAGE GRADIENT	9.5%

MAX GRADIENT
16%

250m
200
150
100
0   500   1000   1500m

BONCELLES
N683
N63
PLAINEVAUX
TILFF
A26
E25
N633
HONY
ESNEUX
N638
4km

BOIS DE FAMELETTE
BOIS DE NOMONT
N633
RUE DE LA ROCHE AUX FAUCONS
BOIS DE MONCEAU
AVENUE D'ESNEUX
F
HONY
D'AVISTER
S

49 Côte de Saint-Nicolas

This is a fantastic climb packed with character. However, twisting its way up through eroding industry and inner city decline it's never going to be the first on your list of roads to visit. It's just not pretty, no matter how hard you look at it and the force required to attack on this slope is as brutal as the environment. Now, I hope my map is good enough – I started up three roads before I finally got the right one. The thing to look for is the railway bridge that sits above the top of the opening straight. Starting on the Rue des Rèwes you ramp up tightly between the houses, there are some gardens on your right then it's up and under the high bridge. From here on the climb is not so claustrophobic and as the road opens up it bends slightly right then rises steeper again, the buildings either side accentuating the gradient. Next the route begins to twist, 90 degrees to the right, then, in front of a row of garages, 90 degrees left. You're now on the Rue Bordelais and the road whips round left then immediately right through a perfect S, and round the base of a tall tower block. You briefly straighten up before plunging into yet another set of bends, tight right then left through more houses to join the final stretch finishing the climb across the white line before the T-junction.

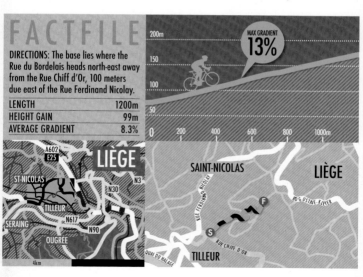

FACTFILE

DIRECTIONS: The base lies where the Rue du Bordelais heads north-east away from the Rue Chiff d'Or, 100 meters due east of the Rue Ferdinand Nicolay.

LENGTH	1200m
HEIGHT GAIN	99m
AVERAGE GRADIENT	8.3%

MAX GRADIENT
13%

𝕾𝕺 𝕮ôte de 𝕬ns

At the end of Liège-Bastogne-Liège, after all that has transpired it comes down to this – one last climb. Here is the point where heroes launch their killer attacks, where legends are created, and dreams are shattered, a place where both glory and despair are tasted in equal measure. You'll find the base at the triangular junction of three roads, and the one you're looking for is the Rue Walthère Jamar. You'll know you're on the right track when you see the giant 'ANS' painted across the smooth surface then repeated every few hundred metres. As you begin, the gradient ramps up incrementally steeper and steeper until you approach the halfway point and a junction with traffic lights. The slope eases a touch here, and if you time your effort right you'll sail through on green to climb steeper again on the other side. There will be a steady flow of traffic all the way up, and some queuing at the lights, but the road is plenty wide enough for neither of these to hinder you or to present any danger. As you ride past the leisure centre the steep slope backs off for a final time before you begin the last push. Now alongside a high brick wall, it's all or nothing. You see the traffic lights on the brow, fix on them and pull yourself upwards, and once you reach them your task is complete.

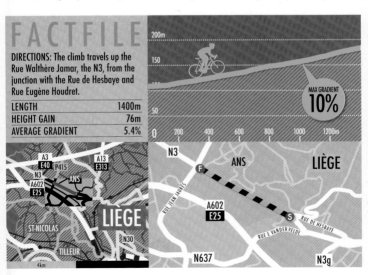

FACTFILE

DIRECTIONS: The climb travels up the Rue Walthère Jamar, the N3, from the junction with the Rue de Hesbaye and Rue Eugène Houdret.

LENGTH	1400m
HEIGHT GAIN	76m
AVERAGE GRADIENT	5.4%

MAX GRADIENT
10%

Tick

So here are the three most important pages of the book: the checklist. It's now time for you to head out and ride the climbs for yourself, follow in the footsteps of the legends and punish your body and bike across the length and breadth of Belgium. Although throughout the book I've not logged a time for each climb, I've included a column in the checklist for you to enter your best effort, so give it 100% and enjoy.

Flanders

NO	CLIMB	DATE RIDDEN	MY TIME
1	KEMMELBERG		
2	RODEBERG + BANEBERG		
3	NOKEREBERG		
4	KLUISBERG		
5	KNOKTEBERG / CÔTE DE TRIEU		
6	OUDE KWAREMONT		
7	PATERBERG		
8	KORTEKEER		
9	KOPPENBERG		
10	OUDE KRUISBERG		
11	LADEUZE		
12	KATTENBERG		
13	VOLKEGEMBERG		

NO	CLIMB	DATE RIDDEN	MY TIME
14	EIKENBERG		
15	TAAIENBERG		
16	KANARIEBERG		
17	BOIGNEBERG		
18	FOREEST		
19	MOLENBERG		
20	LEBERG		
21	VALKENBERG		
22	TENBOSSE		
23	BERENDRIES		
24	MUUR-KAPELMUUR		
25	BOSBERG		

Wallonia

NO	CLIMB	DATE RIDDEN	MY TIME
26	CÔTE DE HAUT-BOIS		
27	CÔTE DE GROYNNE		
28	CÔTE DE PEU D'EAU		
29	CÔTE DE BOHISSEAU		
30	CÔTE DE EREFFE		

31	MUR DE HUY		
32	LES ENCLAVES		
33	VIELLE ROUTE DE FRANCE		
34	CÔTE DE LA ROCHE-EN-ARDENNE		
35	COL DE HAUSSIRE		
36	CÔTE DE SAINT-ROCH		
37	CÔTE DE LA VECQUÉE		
38	CÔTE DE WANNE		
39	CÔTE D'AISÔMONT		
40	CÔTE DE BRUME		
41	CÔTE DE STOCKEU		
42	CÔTE DE LA HAUTE LEVÉE		
43	MONT RIGI		
44	COL DU ROSIER		
45	COL DU MAQUISARD		
46	MONT THEUX		
47	CÔTE DE LA REDOUTE		
48	CÔTE DE LA ROCHE AUX FAUCONS		
49	CÔTE DE SAINT-NICOLAS		
50	CÔTE DE ANS		

Thank you

The list of those involved in this project is short and sweet but it would've been impossible without their help and support. First of course, I'd like to thank my wife and daughter, but wait there just a minute, shouldn't they be thanking me? Thanking me for taking them to see these famous roads, not to mention taking them to The Tour of Flanders Museum in Oudenaard, I know they loved that! Next thanks to my other travelling companion Nick Burton for joining me on one of the research trips. It was his first to Belgium and his first taste of cobbles, steak frites and Duval, I can confirm that the worm has certainly turned for him. We'll never forget that mad afternoon in October looking for a bar to watch the end of the World Road Race Championships, desperate to see Mark Cavendish win the rainbow bands for Great Britain we almost began knocking on doors as bar after bar drew a blank. In the end we resorted to following the action on Twitter, not quite front row seats but at least we felt some of the excitement.

Thanks to Mum and Dad for the loan of the car, and my sister for yet again cross checking my facts and figures. Also thanks to Gordon Knight for passing his eyes over some of my text, it was essential. Thanks to Andy Waterman, Stuart Clapp and Simon Gilbert for sorting me out with a Garmin which was beyond useful on foreign shores and thanks to Frances Lincoln for their continued support.

And finally, and most importantly, I'd like to thank my liquid friends Leffe, Westmalle, Chimay, Orval, Duvel, Kwak...

THE END